THE SPECIAL YEARS

Val Doonican was born in Waterford in Ireland in 1927. He has to his credit: nine hit records, six bestselling LPs, three Television Personality of the Year awards, box office records for theatres all over the country and an annual series of television shows on BBC 1, in addition to a number of special programmes. His main hobby is golf and he lives in Buckinghamshire with his wife, Lynn, and his two daughters, Sarah and Fiona.

The Special Years

An autobiography

VAL DOONICAN

SPHERE BOOKS LIMITED
30/32 Gray's Inn Road, London WC1X 8JL

First published in Great Britain by
Elm Tree Books/Hamish Hamilton 1980
Text and drawings copyright © by Val Doonican 1980
Drawings by Val Doonican
Published by Sphere Books Ltd 1981

Set in Baskerville

Printed and bound in Great Britain by
Cox & Wyman Ltd, Reading

To both my families, old and new,
and to the entire cast of this book

Contents

Introduction

I hope you won't think I sound too Irish when I tell you that I've decided to begin my story – where many of you might expect it to end – at the LONDON PALLADIUM. I do this, so that I might set the scene for what came earlier which, in this case, will come later. That really does sound Irish!

The year was 1970 and I was proud indeed to be starring at that great theatre in my own show – a show that was to run for six months. Things couldn't have been better, really: playing to packed houses and having the added pleasure of sleeping in my own bed every night – an experience I'd rarely known, having done most of my seasonal work in the provinces.

The full houses were, of course, a direct result of the success of my television shows which had been a regular event on BBC since 1964. I was also fortunate enough to have a string of hit records to my credit.

Now, as if all that were not enough for one man, yet another feather was about to be added to those already adorning my Irish cap. I was informed, by my manager, that some very influential gentlemen from ABC television in America were coming to the show in the hope of confirming their belief that I was worth signing-up.

The outcome of their visit was an invitation to record thirteen sixty-minute shows to be transmitted all over the United States and distributed to practically every country in the English speaking world. It was all agreed upon and we were to start work on the shows just as soon as my Palladium season came to an end.

Now, I'd like to take you forward quite a few months, to find the majority of the shows in the can and my wife

1

Lynn and I in New York, on what was called 'a promotion trip', in the spring of 1971.

Our luxurious suite at the Saint Regis Hotel, in the heart of the city, was ablaze with flowers and awash with champagne. Gifts of all shapes and sizes arrived at regular intervals – accompanied by messages of goodwill – from the network, record company, friends and well-wishers. The whole thing felt more like our wedding day.

Having unpacked, freshened-up and tried, without success, to have a snooze (the excitement of the whole thing, coupled with jet-lag, made the latter impossible), we sat down to some afternoon tea.

'Enjoy your meal and welcome to New York,' said the waiter as he left the room, then – turning to my wife – added, 'Happy shoppin', lady!' Poor man, he obviously hadn't looked at our schedule for the week!

Tickets to see Lauren Bacall in 'Applause, Applause' that evening on Broadway, were placed beside a beautiful box of chocolates on Lynn's pillow. 'What a shame,' she said, 'you're doing the David Frost show tonight. We won't be able to make it.' I told her that David's show was quite early and we might get to the theatre in time. Although, to be honest, a Broadway show was not very high on my list of priorities at that particular moment.

About an hour later, the desk clerk rang to say that, 'Mister Doogan's limousine was out front and ready to take him to the studio.' The waiting limousine, we discovered, was big enough to take *ten* Mister Doogans, to those same studios, a few blocks away.

David treated me like a king that evening. He gave me such a build-up – convincing both his studio audience and the millions of viewers that, even though they didn't know me from Adam, they were in for a great treat. You can just imagine what I felt like, sitting there, smiling all over my face, and hoping my host wouldn't overdo it. I felt quite terrified.

My appearance was well received, and I left the stage feeling happy and considerably relieved.

2

By the way, we did manage to creep into that Broadway show and, whether I'd had enough excitement for one night or not, I cannot say, but – I can't remember a thing about it!

We rounded off the day with supper at the famous Sardi's restaurant where, between mouthfuls, I was interviewed by a lady from one of the New York papers.

The rest of the week continued to be a frantic succession of interviews, TV appearances and record sessions, culminating with the Dick Cavett Show in New York and the Mike Douglas Show in Philadelphia.

The highlight of the trip, however, was provided by my sister, Nancy, who has lived in Philadelphia since I was a young lad still at school. (I remember, as if it was yesterday, the time she packed her bags and set off to become a G.I. bride.) She had followed my career with the aid of newspaper cuttings and records sent to her by other members of the Doonican family and now, for the first time, she was to see her kid brother in action.

She sat in the front row as I did the Mike Douglas Show and I couldn't help feeling that the memories reflected in Nancy's smile, painted a pretty fair picture of the long road that I'd travelled since my childhood, back in Waterford, on the south coast of Ireland.

1 The Pram Crash

'John,' I heard my mother call out, 'take that young fella down town and get him a hair cut. You'll find sixpence on the sideboard.' I hated having to go to the barbers and know that most young lads, in those days, looked upon it much as they would having a tooth out.

Our local barber was aware of this, I'm sure, because he rewarded his young customers with a penny as they left the shop and at the same time, he'd pat their newly groomed heads, praising them for good behaviour and bravery in the face of danger.

My brother John held my overcoat by its lapels while I climbed into it and we headed for the front door.

I was about six or seven years old at the time, and my bigger brothers seemed to find it irritating having to match my walking pace whenever they took me out. So John decided on a plan of action that would make life a little easier.

One of our household possessions at that time was an old pram with very strange looking wheels. They looked just as if they were made from bamboo: quite like those you see on fancy tea-trolleys nowadays. The pram was rolled on to the pavement outside the front door and I was instructed to climb aboard, 'with my back to the engine', as it were; John then leaned foward, took hold of the armrests and, with his left foot resting on the axle, used the other one 'scooter style' to set us off down the road – for all the world like a couple of guys starting a bob-sleigh run.

Pretty soon we were moving along at a cracking pace and, as we headed down the hill towards town, John finally jumped aboard, both his feet now firmly planted on the axle. I can almost feel that wonderful glow of exhilaration as the wind whizzed past my ears, eyes glued to my brother's face, while he encouraged us along by making weird engine noises under his breath: Ngaaaaaah ... rhummmmm ... rhummmmmm ... he whined, as our craft careered down Newtown – our speed increasing by the second.

I don't really know what happened next. Maybe we bumped over a manhole, skidded on wet leaves, or my brother's enthusiasm simply reached breaking point but, suddenly, that look of ecstasy that shone from his eyes turned to sheer panic as he lost his foothold. His feet hit the road just behind the pram, causing his head to shoot forward into my stomach. Desperately he tried to hang on – but in vain. I watched the back of his head as it went sliding over my knees, then his chin slowly pulled my socks down to my ankles till, finally, with one last desperate lurch, he was gone. I left him, lying spread-eagled in the middle of the road, as my machine and I sped on, 'driverless'.

You can imagine my situation! I had no earthly way of stopping the thing. I couldn't turn round to see where I was going. In fact, I was so completely petrified that I sat, motionless, except for my eyeballs, which flashed from side to side, first to the left then to the right, exchanging glances with each passer-by. One by one, people stopped in their tracks, slowly turned round on the spot, and stared speechlessly as I flashed by and disappeared into the distance.

My local knowledge told me that at the bottom of the hill this particular road was skirted by the wall of our city park. It was a very low wall and I worked out that, from the angle at which my vehicle was moving, the park wall would indeed by my final destination. I didn't bother to shout for help. In fact, by now, I had simply accepted that I was about to reach my final end, at the age of six and a half, as the victim of a 'pram crash'.

And what a pram crash it turned out to be! When at last the front wheels hit the little kerb, the pram simply leaped into the air and, with a sickening crash, collided with the wall. I in turn took off from my seat and head first went slithering over the park wall, disappearing down the other side like a snake into a hole. I landed on my head on a cinder-covered pathway just inside and, for a moment, all was still as I lay there – stunned; my poor head tingling from the effects of the cinders.

'Are y'alright, boy?', John said as he stood over me, gently helping me to my feet. I don't know if I answered but I do know that, shortly afterwards, I was seated on a little plank of wood perched across the armrest of the barber's chair (for the benefit of the 'little people') each stroke of the comb and snip of the scissors bringing tears to my eyes. My brother sat on the bench behind me, watching the reflection of my agonies in the mirror. Whenever I dared to take a peek and caught his eye, he would smile a wicked smile, slowly raising a threatening fist as if to say, 'Don't you dare say it hurts or we'll both get into trouble and, what's more, you won't get your penny.'

At the risk of sounding smug, I think I should tell you that I sat through the ordeal without a whimper. I got my reward and I've never told a soul. I think the pram was a write-off though!

When I think about the early part of my life, my first thoughts are of my home. I started life at No. 10, Passage Road, in Waterford. Number 10 was one end of a group of four houses or, to be more precise, it was the last quarter of a long, narrow, single-storey building with four front doors, four front windows and one long slated roof with skylights giving a glimmer of light to the attic rooms.

Since our front door led directly on to the pavement, the only garden space was a tiny strip at the back. We also had a little backyard with two outhouses. One was a garden shed, which held the turf for the fire and dad's gardening tools, the other was a toilet. A tap on the wall outside the back door, was our only running water; we never enjoyed the luxury of a kitchen sink or a bathroom.

Passage Road
No. 10 is fourth on the left

Dad had built an extension at the rear of the house, which we called the back-kitchen: a flat-roofed affair that looked out into the yard and garden. He kept the garden looking like a picture, with a beautiful show of flowers on either side of the narrow path which lead to the summer-house-type building at the bottom. This was known as 'The Hut' and was to play a very big part in my childhood.

The house itself had four rooms, two up and two down. Upstairs was really nothing more than an attic with a dividing partition creating two bedrooms: one for girls and one for boys. The stairs were originally a simple set of steps by the wall; these too had been neatly boxed in by my father and a wooden door shut them off from the room below.

The front room, or parlour as it was then called, was

where my parents slept for the best part of my young life and the last remaining room was where we really lived. We spent the greater part of our indoor lives in that crowded little place, with its cold stone floor and assorted furniture. The centre piece was a large kitchen table, which the girls took turns to scrub and which my mother never failed to grace with something delicious to eat. By the wall, under the window, was one of those sofas that always looked as if it had an arm missing. Against the opposite wall was our wind-up gramophone on a small table and, beside that, was an old Singer sewing machine that had to be worked with the feet. It was covered with one of those dome shaped lids, underneath which you might expect to see a steaming joint of beef. Our selection of family chairs were usually to be found surrounding the open fireplace and on the wall hung our lovely old wooden clock, which chimed its way through the first twenty years of my life.

The short hallway leading to the front door was bare except for a simple octagonal table which usually held a plant pot of some kind. In the corner by the front door, Dad had made a little cabinet – the sole purpose of which was to hide the gas meter.

At a very early age I'd noticed a line of little holes in the old plaster on the 'gable end' side of the hall; they were tiny craters about an inch in diameter, the origin of which makes quite a romantic anecdote.

Back in the Black and Tan days of the 1918–20s, the citizens of Ireland were subjected to quite rigid nightly curfews compelling them, among other things, to be indoors at a specified time. My father went out one night to lock up before retiring, when he heard a commotion in the street outside. A neighbour had been spotted by snipers concealed behind the wall of the hospital grounds across the road. He was instructed to 'halt' and identify himself but, whatever his response was, he was greeted with a hail of bullets. He dashed to take shelter in our hallway – and left us with this relic. Many were the times I stood there poking my fingers into those little holes, watching as a trickle of white dust sprinkled to the floor like talcum powder.

Everybody knew everybody else in our thickly-populated neighbourhood and, if you didn't have plenty of friends, you had only yourself to blame.

The rent man made his rounds at regular intervals, to collect his dues and sign the book. I think our house cost something like a shilling a week (that's five pence, today). It was an old house and rather cold, as indeed were most of those old houses, but my mother kept it warm with her love and kindness – and I don't think I've known a happier place!

My mother was a most attractive woman, always smiling and happy, and completely unselfish in her devotion to the family. Like most working-class mothers, living under the conditions of the day, she never seemed to worry about herself or what she got from life. It's not difficult to imagine the problems she faced daily, bringing up eight children and coping with all the other chores that running our little home entailed. Come to think of it, I always felt we were quite well-off compared with many of the other families in our neighbourhood and I realise now that the feeling of security stemmed, almost entirely, from my mother's amazing talents for making ends meet. As for her beloved brood of eight; perhaps I should give you a brief introduction to them all.

First there was my brother Ned, whose life was really removed from mine as he was nearing marrying age before I could chat to him about anything other than conkers or Cowboys and Indians. He did love sport, though, and took me to lots of games at our local grounds and, since I've become a man, we've grown very close and I always look forward to our meetings.

Then came Mary, who was the member of the family I knew least about. She died when I was very young and had been ill for some time previously, so I can't say that I ever had the opportunity of getting to know her.

Next in line, John, who was the extrovert of the family but – I've already told you about him. Then Lar; a gentle man who, like Ned, Mary and my other sister, Nancy, had beautiful auburn hair. He too was plagued with illness for a great part of his life and, regretfully, that's how I remember him. He died in 1950.

The fifth arrival in the family, Nellie, was the busy bee of the house – dashing off to work, dashing home again. She loved to spend her spare time singing in church choirs, in amateur musical groups, and so on.

Nancy also was involved in all kinds of musical activites and, like Nellie, got tremendous pleasure from the company of her colleagues. She now lives in the United States with her family, as I've already told you, but she visits us almost every year.

Finally, Una, only a couple of years older than me and the closeness of our ages reflected itself in the warmth of our relationship. We were terrific pals and spent endless hours just enjoying each other's company.

I am No. 8, of course; and all of us together, have put my mother in line for some kind of record by giving her thirty-five grandchildren with great-grandchildren, slowly but surely, approaching the same number. I was, in fact, christened *Michael* Valentine Doonican – 'Valentine' was added because my birthday is 3 February, not far from St Valentine's Day, and so I was given the added protection of a second saint. However, as our neighbourhood was absolutely overrun with Michaels, Micks, Mickeys and Mikes, I was called Val for convenience and easy identification.

My father died, quite tragically, when I was a boy of fourteen. In spite of the fact that I didn't spend a great period of my life in his company he, nevertheless, made an enormous impression on me. This, strangely enough, seems to mature with the years – like a good wine.

He was a shortish man with a completely bald head and one of those moustaches that he could comb for special occasions – sharpening both ends with 'spitty' thumbs and forefingers. He had bandy legs and I can almost see him now, coming up the road from work, looking a bit like Tom Mix. He carried one of those folded metal rules, which protruded from the leg pocket of his overall – swinging about like a six-gun as he approached.

One of the pleasures I learned to enjoy in his company was walking. He thought nothing of a seven- or eight-mile walk on a Sunday, my age at that time being on a par with the distance. I loved it. He had a ritual he liked to follow on these occasions.

We'd call at the corner shop, where he would buy a pennyworth of sweets. Having placed them in the pocket of his jacket, or overcoat, he would open a book and, with his glasses perched on the end of his nose, walk along the middle of the road by sheer instinct as he read. (He was an avid reader, something I didn't inherit from him and one of my regrets.)

'Don't walk in the middle of the road,' I remember saying to him, 'you'll get run over by a car.'

'That's where you're wrong, son,' he answered with a smile and, still reading, 'It's when you walk on the side of the road that you get run over!'

I've often said, in fun, that when they put white lines on the road anywhere within ten miles of my home, they simply painted in my father's footsteps.

When I needed nourishment from time to time on our journey, I'd simply help myself to a sweet from his pocket, then continue my explorations through the fields and woods, keeping in touch with his progress by watching his bowler hat as it bobbed along above the hedges. Sometimes we'd take along slices of bread and butter sprinkled with salt then, resting on the bank of a fresh country stream, we'd pick watercress and make sand-wiches. Watercress has never tasted quite the same since!

My father, 'liked his drink', as they say in Ireland. Many's the hour I have spent waiting outside pubs on the road near Knockboy or Grantstown drinking fizzy lemonade which he'd brought out to me. When it was

11

gone I'd pass the time away by either making mud pies in the glass or wandering round to the back of the pub where they had hens, pigs and cattle. It was at times like those that I began to learn the precious accomplishment of how to amuse myself.

One of my favourite Irish stories, is the one about a visitor driving along a country road. He got behind an old farm tractor and followed it for a mile or so, desperately trying to find an opportunity to overtake. When, finally, he decided to have a go at getting by, the tractor, without any kind of indication, turned right and went through a gateway. The poor driver of the car swerved to avoid a collision and finished up in the ditch. In a rage, he climbed out of his car and charged up to the old farmer who was closing the gate.

'You fool!' he shouted. 'What the hell do you think you're doing? Turning right like that, you could have killed me!'

The tractor driver looked amazed ... 'What do you mean?' he said ... 'You should have waited ... sure, everybody round here knows that *I'm* goin' to turn in that gate!'

That just about sums up how things were when I was a boy. Everybody knew everybody else and where they lived. One little trick of my father's that always impressed me, was his ability to walk for some seven miles, as I described, never taking his eyes off the book, but saying 'hello' to everybody. He knew who would be where, at what time and, above all, he got his greeting right ...

'Hello, Mary ... is the young lad better now?'

'Mornin', Mick ... get the job done in time?'

'How are the asters comin' along, Alice?'

He had an absolute passion for flowers and grew them with enviable success. He did it for the right reasons, too, in my opinion: simply to look at, or to give to people who didn't have a garden.

One of my earliest memories is sitting on the ground in the garden, squeezing the head of an antirrhinum between

12

my thumb and forefinger watching its little pink mouth open and close, and, at the same time, quizzing my father on the names of the various blooms.

'Why do thay all have different smells?' I asked, pressing the antirrhinum against my nose.

He gave me a long, serious look. 'The smells come from the sweets that grow in each flower.'

There was no answer to that, so I waited for more. He leaned forward, pointing to a yellowish one, 'Now this is an aster and it will grow a Rainbow Toffee . . . This one is called a lupin and it's where barley sugar comes from . . . Wallflowers here, they grow aniseed balls.'

I said nothing but couldn't help looking forward to a good crop.

The lovely thing is, he didn't forget what he had told me and was well aware of how I might await the results.

He was dead right too! I even invited some of my pals to the harvest, which he announced some weeks later. Making sure we were standing well back, so as not to tread on his precious plants, he performed the most impressive sleight of hand, shaking flowers at random and casually handing us the spoils.

You can well imagine the effect it had on us kids. It is not surprising he became known in our street, as 'The Sweet Man'.

My mother assures me that my father 'never laid a hand on any of us' and I quite believe it. Yet he did punish me for any blatant breach of the rules. I remember being in the doghouse, one time, for having a row with my sister and pushing her down some stairs. It was on a Friday and when he came in from work we were having dinner in the usual way when, quite casually, as we all sat round the table chatting, he said, 'What's this I hear about you knocking your sister over today, boy?' I had a strange sinking feeling but knew there was no point in beating about the bush. I owned-up. I was looking forward to going to the pictures next day and frankly feared the worst. It came, too!

13

'When you've finished your meal now, go up to your room and don't come down till Mass on Sunday.'

I did as I was told, without protest.

He came to see me on numerous occasions during my internment and, whenever I came down to the toilet, which as I've said was outside in the yard, he'd smile, have a chat, then off I'd go, back to my cell.

My room, which I shared with my brothers, was very small and, without them, very lonely. Like any attic it came to a point above your head – in this case, where the roof met the wooden partition separating it from the other half. I lay on the bed, looking straight up at the sky through the skylight above me. Pasted to the wall, around my bed, were a few pictures of my favourite film heroes – stolen from my sisters' movie magazines.

The only other furniture in the room, apart from our beds, was a small chest-of-drawers and a home-made bedside table. On the table, at arm's length, were my simple aids to passing the hours of confinement: drawing-book and pencil, which have continued to be at hand throughout my life, as you will see from the pictures in this book, *Beano Annual*, one *Hotspur* comic, two *Champions* and a small cardboard box containing some personal treasures.

From time to time I climbed up to take a look at the outside world, my head peeping through the skylight – now opened as wide as it would go. Across the road, in the grounds of the County Hospital, an old man was digging potatoes, quite unaware of my plight, while on the wind I heard laughing voices as my pals went about their games just round the corner in St Alphonsus Road, a few houses to my right.

When, at last, my term of punishment was over, Dad just said, 'Good lad,' and the matter was never mentioned again – or forgotten, by the prisoner.

Through my young life, and indeed my career, in common with everybody else, I've constantly seen situations where people in authority – whether parents or employers – have made rules, seen them broken, then not carried out the threatened punishment. I think this is one of the greatest weaknesses in a parent-child relationship.

Here's another example of what rules meant to my dad. When I was about seven years old I got my first bout of real sickness. Well, at least it was the first illness for which I was sent to hospital.

All I can remember about the symptoms is the skin beginning to peel off the soles of my feet; not that it's a complete summing up of what it feels like to have scarlet fever, I'm sure. However, there was great excitement and sense of occasion in No. 10, as my little suitcase was packed and the sad 'Goodbyes' almost enjoyed by one and all.

My mother had been very worried about me and knew that my going away was the only cure. What I didn't realise was, that this particular ailment required the patient to be isolated from the outside world! It was really awful not being able to have visitors for about seven weeks. My family made regular visits to the hospital, however, and waved and talked to me through a large window at the end of the ward. My sister, Una, made faces and ate sweets and I drooled like Pluto the dog. I managed to pass a lot of the time by drawling little pictures and proudly held up my work to the window for my fans to admire during each visiting session.

As I neared the end of my confinement, my father asked me if there was anything I'd like to celebrate my home-coming. Among my sketches was one outlining my idea of the ultimate in trolleys, or scooters, or whatever you call a plank of wood fitted with some old pram wheels and steered by means of a piece of rope used to drag the front axle from side to side. This particular model had such extras as fitted seats, headlamps made from empty tins, number plates and – would you believe – a steering wheel. Without hesitation, my father took the details of my design and, with a kind of grin that I've never seen

15

anybody else use to such effect, gave me the thumbs-up sign.

Two weeks later, with great excitement and relief, I received the news that I was ready to go home. To show how times have changed, I recall the fact that there was no family transport. We couldn't afford to hire any so my journey home, which was only a few blocks anyway, was achieved sitting on my brother John's shoulders, wearing my warm overcoat – and a muffler, belonging to my grandmother.

Mother had prepared a wonderful tea with all my favourites, including jam fritters and tarts of every denomination. The room glowed with the heat of a generous fire. Later, when all the excitement had died down, everybody was busily chatting and the attention had left yours truly, my father caught my eye and beckoned me towards the hall door. I followed him into the hall, then turned into the front room. There, in the middle of the floor, was the most exciting present I have ever had.

He had built *my* trolley, complete with not only all my additional suggestions, but quite a few of his own inspired ideas, making it look like something by da Vinci. I really was speechless and couldn't wait to test-drive it up and down the hall. How I looked forward to getting it outside and showing it off to my friends.

Now, in the midst of the excitement, I well remember my father saying, 'I want you to promise me you won't go on that footpath and possibly hurt somebody.' He was worried that, since the houses had no front gardens, I would go straight from the front door on to the footpath, making it very easy to knock somebody over. I made my promise; to which he added, 'Mind now, if you don't do as I've told you, I'll take it from you!'

We had a ball with that toy for a long, long time until one day, as you've probably guessed, we went belting down the next street – on the footpath – simply because we liked the sound of the flagstones under the wheels. They sounded a bit like the points on the railway track. (I think

I should mention that, in those days, cars were so few and far between that it was very safe to go on the road. The occasional oncoming car was so noisy, you heard it long before it presented any danger.) Well, the worst happened: a lady stepped out carrying a shopping bag and immediately tried to jump out of our way. Luckily, we only knocked her back against the wall – leaving her a bit shaken, but unhurt.

I knew that, in a small community like ours, the news would soon get back to my dad. It was next day at lunch when the crunch came. In his usual casual way, without a sign of aggression, he said, 'Are you going to tell me about Mrs Deegan, then?' I knew I was cornered. I looked at him and smiled, told him what happened and, believe it or not, I never saw the trolley again! Some days later I saw the wheels tied together with string hanging up in the garden shed.

I suppose you could say his actions were a bit extreme as it was only a first offence but then, I had the choice of doing right or wrong, and I chose wrong. Through my childhood I learned to accept the consequences. He comes to my mind so many times when I fail to follow through my own rules at home. I'm convinced that children look upon it as a sign of weakness and would prefer it if you punished them as you'd threatened.

Up to now, you've probably got the impression that I hero-worshipped my father – this if far from the truth. I knew, at a very early age, that he drank too much; he spent too much of his hard-earned and our badly needed money gambling on the horses; and he smoked non-stop. I can't say he chain-smoked because, in fact, he smoked an old clay pipe which was brown with age. His tobacco was the plug type which he cut with his penknife and kneaded between the palms of his calloused hands. He also chewed tobacco, just like the old characters in the Westerns.

I was always very aware of the tension caused by his drinking and the subsequent shortage of money. I doubt if my mother ever got used to it, or learned to accept him when he showed signs of having had too much. Saturday

17

was usually a bad time. Having finished work at 12.30, he'd go for some drinks with the boys. My mother would prepare his lunch and, far too often, it would still be there two or three hours later. On occasions, I would have to go and look for him; I knew which pubs he favoured and would stick my head round the door of each one in turn, shouting, 'Is me dad here?' In those very early days I developed a dislike for pubs that I've never lost. The smell of the beer and the smoke and sawdust on the floor may have been heaven to the old boys at the bar but, to me, it was ugly and depressing.

Even now, when I play clubs around the world, I sometimes feel a strange twinge of revulsion when I smell the drinks and the smoke. My father would leave the pub with me and walk out into the daylight, wiping his moustache with the back of his hand, and carrying under his arm a week's supply of books – which usually numbered about six. He read all night long, from what I could gather.

As my own bedroom lighting was limited to one candlepower, I never went in for reading in bed very much. I'd just lie and count the stars directly above my head – I refer to the ones in the sky, not the film stars I stole from my sister's movie magazine.

One night during the war I sat bolt upright in bed when I heard, what sounded like an approaching aircraft; a rare noise to our ears since Ireland wasn't involved in the war. The others hadn't come upstairs yet so, climbing up on to the end of my bed, I looked out through my observation tower – my eyes twitching in the cold night air. Then I spotted it. The faint flashing lights of, what I was now possitive was, a low flying aircraft, flickered closer. It went thundering over the rooftops, its engines spluttering and obviously in trouble. This much I'd become familiar with from the many war films at our local cinema. Then, in a second, it was gone from my view. I didn't move, just listened as the horrible engine sounds faded into the night. Suddenly, I had my first experience of the sound of

18

silence, absolute silence – and it was loud.

Next morning, news was about town that a German bomber had lost its bearings and gone the wrong way, finishing up in a ploughed field a couple of miles from my home. Naturally, it created enormous interest in Waterford. Most of the local people went on foot, or bicycle, to have a look. With lots of bits and pieces of wreckage about the place, souvenirs were plentiful. I treasured a tiny piece of metal, with a wire attached to one end, for years afterwards. We were informed that the crew were safe and had been sent away – to wherever such people are sent on these occasions.

The pop-fan of the family, in the earlier days, was my brother John. He followed all the top singers of the time with great interest, his hero was that young man of song, Bing Crosby. His fanatical enthusiasm nearly drove my father mad for, try as he might, he simply couldn't share John's avid appreciation of the old 'groaner'.

'For God's sake, will ya' shut that fella off,' Dad would groan as John turned the radio up a notch. 'He sounds like a bloody calf, with his moanin'.'

John was my idol as a boy. He really was great fun, teasing me constantly but, like my dad, unstinting with his time. I'd wait patiently at the front door, each evening, once I'd heard the 'knock-off' hooter announcing his homeward journey.

I was painfully thin as a child, a bit taller than most of my playmates, with legs sticking out of my baggy shorts like a couple of 'five irons'. Even in those days, my crooked teeth smiled from beneath my blonde fringe. One of John's party pieces was to encircle my twig-like wrist with his thumb and forefinger then, with one sharp movement and a loud 'Tarrah', he'd slide his right hand up to my armpits and down again – without parting his fingertips. At least, so he claimed, whenever he gave one of his frequent demonstrations to all and sundry. My affection for him was a standing joke in the family – and whenever they

19

saw John, they could be sure I wasn't far behind.

One evening I watched him pour a kettle of hot water into the enamel basin on the back-kitchen table, in preparation for a shave. 'Now, stand back,' he warned, 'and don't let me see you fiddlin' with anything, OK?' I moved away, with my hands behind my back and just stood there, staring. He began to soap his whiskers, at the time singing one of Bing's latest hits. 'Love thy neighbour, walk up and say, how be ya' ... boo, boo, boo, boo ... and get me a clean towel ... boo, boo, boo.'

I disappeared and returned, in seconds, carrying a neatly folded, crispy, clean towel still warm from airing in front of the fire. I put it on the table beside him, then, hoping he wouldn't notice, decided to stand my ground. He didn't seem to mind, so I thought it safe to sneak a look at his jar of Brylcreem. Silently, I slid it off the table and began to unscrew its shiny black lid. It worked, and there I was, in a world of my own, my finger testing the lovely creamy white stuff that smelled just like he did.

I was wearing my large shorts at the time, held up by an even larger pair of braces. The next thing I remember, was a hand grabbing those braces just between my shoulder blades and lifting me clean into the air. He stood glaring at me like the Incredible Hulk, his voice booming in mock anger, 'Didn't I tell you not to fiddle?' he roared into my face. My trousers got tighter between my legs, till I felt as if I'd slipped-off a bicycle saddle on to the crossbar.

Slowly and deliberately he walked towards the back door then, with both hands holding my braces, by now stretched over my head, he allowed me to slide gradually down the door, till the braces reached the huge coat hook.

Looping the elastic over the hook, he dramatically backed away, never taking his eyes off mine. 'Now, I'm going to a dance,' he hissed through his teeth. 'And you will stay right where you are, till I get home at two o'clock in the morning.' He dried his face, slipped on his coat and disappeared, leaving me hanging on the door like an old scarecrow.

In seconds he was back, laughing his head off and bringing the rest of the family to join in the fun. 'God bless us, and save us,' said my mother, coming to my rescue, 'you could do the child an injury.'

I laughed as much as anybody else, despite the discomfort and – thank goodness – it didn't affect my singing voice!

Only when John had gone out with his pals, would I sit by the fire and tackle the job of amusing myself. It was a real bonus for me when, for some reason, he decided to spend an evening at home. Poor devil, I must have pestered the life out of him.

2 'These Boots were made for Walking'

I had my own special seat by the fire. So close to the fire, in fact, that it was virtually inside the cavity in the wall where our fire burned. My private stool was made from an upturned margarine case and my mother made it more comfortable with the addition of a cushion. I was never happier than when I was tucked away in my corner with a copy of *Beano*, or *Dandy*, which I read to the accompaniment of the family's normal activities. We ate, talked, read, played music, listened to the radio, used the sewing machine, did the ironing and many other things, all in that one room. You learned to close your eyes and ears to anything that didn't concern you.

When my mother set the table for meals, Dad's chair was situated in such a way that we sat back-to-back when I was on my stool. I can still smell his oily overalls, mingled with the fumes of his pipe and his beer. Sometimes, if he was eating alone, he would slip his hand behind him and nudge me. When I looked round, I'd come face to face with his dinner fork, bearing a tasty piece of his meat, pointing towards my mouth like the beak of a mother bird feeding its young.

One day, I remember sitting there and noticing a strange smell coming from the table. I took a peep around my father's arm to find him stirring his teacup, he then proceeded to drink this odd-smelling brew.

My curiosity got the better of me, so I enquired, 'What's that awful smelly stuff, Dad?' Between swigs, he said, 'Coffee.'

Since I'd never tasted coffee I took his word for it, but couldn't help wondering how it came to be so popular while giving-off such a foul smell.

'Wanta drop?' he asked.

'Don't think so,' I mumbled, hoping he wouldn't press the matter.

'Go on,' he said, 'try it. It won't poison you.'

When the cup reached my face the smell was infinitely worse, but I couldn't be a coward. Trying to look nonchalant I took a generous gulp and cannot remember, before or since, tasting anything quite so foul! I suppose I was about ten years old at the time and it wasn't until ten years later that I found out the truth about my father's brew.

I was dining with my mother at a Dublin restaurant. When the waitress suggested coffee at the end of the meal, my mother said, 'Yes, please,' and as my usual reaction was to refuse – remembering my father's concoction – I hesitated for a second then, to be sociable, I took my life in my hands and said, 'Yes, coffee for two, please.'

The coffee was poured and, without a great deal of enthusiasm, I took my first sip. My taste buds were ready to revolt because of past experience but, to my astonishment, I found it quite palatable.

'This is not bad, is it?' I remarked to my mother. 'I'm quite surprised ... I like it.'

My mother looked up: 'Don't you like coffee, then?' she asked quite innocently.

'Well, I didn't,' I said. 'The last coffee I tasted was some of Dad's.'

'Your dad's?' she queried, in amazement. 'He didn't drink coffee very much but, whenever he did, it was more likely to be half coffee, half rum.'

'Rum?' I choked. 'No wonder it nearly poisoned me!'

She sat back and laughed till her eyes filled with tears. 'You daft fool,' she said, reaching for a hankie. 'If your father was here, he'd die laughin'.'

Sometimes, when my father worked overtime, he'd invite me to go with him. Usually, on those occasions, the 'works' would be closed so, having got the key from the night watchman, he would simply light-up his own particular workshop and off we'd go. My first job was to get his little furnace going, in preparation for heating up some bars of iron which he had to forge into different shapes.

Even though I was very young, he would show me how the job was done and then ask me if I'd like to have a go. I'd find myself hammering and shaping pieces of 2″ by ¼″ flat iron into something resembling the required design. He always let me think that I knew what I was doing and, most important, that I was being a great help.

It's easy to feel that this is all rather naïve and sentimental, but I believe it's imperative that children feel they are able to make a genuine contribution to helping in the house or other family jobs. We are more inclined, nowadays, to do everything for our children rather than make them feel they can do things for us. I certainly felt very important when I 'helped' and that's something I'm glad I didn't miss; it gave me the confidence to do things on my own later on. Dad never said things like, 'You wouldn't understand,' or, 'I'll tell you when you're older,' when I quizzed him. Instead, he gave me the opportunity of deciding, for myself, whether I could understand – or not.

He loved his work and took a great pride in it. As a structural steelworker with a local firm he built things like large farm buildings, haybarns, etc. His workshop had an expansive floor area where he would design each job with wooden templates, marking the floor by means of a stretched piece of string line which he'd rub over with chalk while it was suspended about a half inch from the ground. Then he'd lift the cord and let it spring back against the ground, leaving a long white line as his mark.

I'm sure, by present day standards, that his workshop would seem rather primitive but to me, as a boy, his various machines for cutting half-inch steel plates or sawing huge steel girders were immensely impressive. In fact when I left school, at the age of eighteen, I finished up working in that same job myself and spent a couple of years toiling over those machines that conjured up such magical memories. But I do know that, if my father was told that I'd gone from school to work there, it would have disappointed him a great deal. Like most fathers, he spent his life doing a job that he felt wouldn't be good enough for his golden-haired boy. Two of my elder brothers, Ned and John, did work there for a long time and I feel, somehow, that my father hoped that I was going to prove the exception.

His ambitions for me were confirmed, to some extent, when we had a long talk just before he died but – I'll come to that later.

Like many working men in those days my father was a very talented do-it-yourself enthusiast; he did all our decorating, made a great deal of our furniture, built the out-houses in the garden and, it was automatically accepted, would do 'ordinary' jobs like building cupboards, garden gates etc. Today, people's requirements have changed. To start with, their demands are usually of a much higher standard and, secondly, they can afford to have their jobs done by professionals. Still, I suppose that life nowadays is so demanding that very few people get time enough, away from their work, to do these kinds of jobs.

A good deal of that 'doing-the-thing-yourself' washed-off on all of us – mainly, because he was always willing and happy to show us how things should be done. I mentioned earlier that we never had money for luxury items, and toys most certainly came under that heading. So I tried to emulate my dad by making my own toys; in fact, I've still got a little carving of a horse's head that I did when I was about nine years old.

There was a carpentry department in the firm where he worked and models were made for the steel department. So, from time to time, he'd pop in there and collect all the various shaped pieces of waste wood piled-up in the sawdust beneath the electric saws. He'd pack them into a large carrier bag and bring them home to me. These old left-overs ranged in shape from circular, oval, half-moon, to square or triangular, and in size from one to six inches. To me, they meant hours of pleasure as I built them into all kinds of fascinating structures.

One evening he brought home a large consignment and, without a moment's hesitation, I emptied the lot on the floor and started on my building activities – oblivious of the fact that my mother would be preparing tea shortly and that this would mean clearing the decks for the table. I was completely absorbed in the designing of something or other, when I heard the 'leaves' going up on the table as my mother started to bring it into the centre of the room.

'Out of the way, love,' she mumbled at me.

'Just a minute, Mum, while I do this,' I answered – hoping she'd go away and knowing she wouldn't.

'Come on,' she said. 'Whatever it is can wait till later.'

I still ignored her and continued with my work. I had about ten pieces of wood perched on each other when, suddenly, a ball of rolled newspaper came hurtling from the fireside and sent the lot flying! In a rage I looked up, only to see the back of my father's head encircled by a halo of pipesmoke and, over his shoulder, I could see the top of his open book.

'Did you do that, Dad?' I asked furiously.

'Of course,' he said. 'If you won't do as your mother asks you, then there's nothing for it but more violent action.' He said all this with his usual wry grin. Well – I wasn't going to be treated like this so, with a bad case of the sulks, I packed away my playthings and said I didn't want any tea. My mother immediately began to make a fuss about it but my father raised his hand and said: 'Leave him be!' I walked into the garden, very much wanting my tea, not knowing how to put things to rights – especially, when nobody came to fetch me back. Which would definitely have happened had my father not been there!

When tea was over I was still in the garden alone and, finally, heard my father's footsteps approaching.

'OK, son?' he asked.

'Umph,' I answered.

'Will you give me a hand with this rubbish,' he said, 'it really is a mess down here.' Reluctantly, I went to the end of the garden and helped him tidy up and pretty soon I was smiling again – and still hungry. When the job was almost done, he turned to me and said, 'Well, that's better, thank you, boy. I'll finish it off now and you go and have your tea.' I washed my hands under the tap in the yard, and sat down to enjoy my tea.

Later, when I came out and found him, he asked, 'Enjoy that?'

'Great,' I answered.

'Did you tell your mother, it was great?' he went on.

'Nope,' I said.

'I think you should, you know, after all, she got it ready twice!'

I shouted my half-hearted thanks through the back door and went and sat on the door step of the hut to talk to him.

'You know, son, you should learn to control that mood of yours; it'll cause you a lot of heartache. If anybody wants to get the better of you, all they have to do is get you a little bit upset and they've got you beaten. I managed to upset you just then – and I don't want to hurt you at all. But, one of these days, you'll find that somebody will really want to hurt you, so you should learn not to put your hurt on show for all to see. Get it out of your system and forget it. Don't sulk!' He was right. It has caused me much heartache and people have upset me too easily.

The ironic thing is, I find myself giving the same advice to my daughters – I hope they learn. It's a valuable piece of information and should be taken seriously. I wonder if, in fact, you can get rid of these emotional weaknesses, or whether it's an integral part of your make-up and you've got to learn to live with it?

On another occasion I was fighting hard, emotionally, to face up to some disappointment or other and, in my mind, I truly felt that the world had crumbled about me. I was walking along the road with my father, both of us silent, when he finally spoke.

'You're really disappointed, aren't you?'

27

'Yeah,' I said.

'Is it all that important?' he asked me. 'Think about it!'

At that moment, we were passing a five-bar gate in a country lane where a very old man was standing with his dog.

My father nudged me and said, quietly, 'Ya see that fella over there.'

I nodded. 'Well, believe it or not, in spite of the fact that you've never seen him before in your life, he thinks the world revolves around him. You think about that!'

I have done, a lot. He wanted me to know that the easiest thing in the world is to get so wrapped-up in yourself, you can forget that other people's lives are just as important to them.

It was about this time that my sister Mary became ill. She had contracted tuberculosis, in a form that was known as 'Galloping Consumption': a type of TB that spreads like wildfire through the lungs, leaving the unfortunate sufferer in the most dreadful physical state.

There was really no way she could be properly accommodated in the upstairs bedroom in this condition, since others had to share with her. It was then that my father decided to move out of the house, and into the hut at the bottom of the garden: the tiny wooden building, barely big enough for his single bed and small table.

Mary, in turn, was moved into the front room where my mother could look after her and from where, with the doors kept ajar, her calls could be heard.

I can't say I recall very much about the period of her confinement. The awful disease was viewed with such horror in those days, that I'm sure my poor mother thought it best if we children stayed away from it as far as possible.

My father's new 'digs', on the other hand, struck me as a great idea, since my young mind linked it with log cabins and bunkhouses; now familiar from visits to the local cinema. Looking back, I dread to think what it was like

The Hut

during the winter weather. I'd sometimes watch him disappear down the garden, one hand holding the flickering oil lamp, the other shielding the glass shade from the night winds. As the door closed behind him and the glow of the lamp flickered at the windows, it never occurred to me how uniniviting the chilly bed must have looked - and felt - on those frosty nights.

Today when such sophisticated possessions as transistor radios, video cassette players and microwave ovens, have become commonplace it's difficult, indeed, to imagine these things from my childhood years. Think of the circumstances in the Doonican household. Our one oil lamp provided the only light, to read, sew, cook, wash, do your homework and everything else. When someone finally left the room to go to bed, they simply took a candle - in a candlestick or stuck to a saucer.

The day arrived, however, when quite a few people in our neighbourhood acquired electric lights. Pretty soon, the members of our household began to feel deprived; so a delegation must have gone to the master who, after a few discouraging remarks, said he'd think about it. He did think about it and, before long, we were given the news that electricity was on the way.

I'll never forget the excitement when it finally happened. I don't quite remember how many bulbs we had but the night of the great 'switch on' in our living-room was on a par with the Blackpool Illuminations. A beautiful sixty watt bulb, hanging from the boarded ceiling, flashed into being and our room was positively snow-white with its brilliance! The luxury of being able to do your 'ecker' (a word we used for homework – an abreviation of exercise) at one end of the room, while your mother was knitting a pair of socks at the other end, was something we never could have anticipated.

One amusing aspect of it all is that, at first, I always waited for my parents to switch on. I felt, somehow, that such a sophisticated acquisition was not for kids. Soon, however, the novelty wore off and all and sundry had a go at it, my mother bought a shade in Woolworths, and our life took on a new chapter!

The next thrill was the wireless. We got one 'on tick' for one shilling a week and I don't think there has ever been such an influence in my life. I adored the radio: the talks, plays, comedy shows, quiz shows, the endless music and, of course, the news. Although, as I mentioned before, Ireland was not in the war, we were so close to it all with the radio in our home.

The nice thing, was how the radio became part of the family: we'd sit around in silence and listen to 'ITMA', 'Bandwagon', 'In Town Tonight', 'Monday Night At Eight', 'Stand Easy', 'Variety Bandbox', 'Happidrome', as if we were in a theatre audience. The delight of having such a superb service at our fingertips was beyond description and I don't think that any kind of entertainment has made the same impact on me since then. I loved jazz but couldn't afford to buy records, so I would look up the radio shows, many of them not at peak listening times, and often had the radio all to myself.

Around this period lots of music 'happened' in our home: my brother John played the mandolin quite well, as did my Uncle Larry who lived round the corner. They had many get-togethers when we'd listen to them playing waltzes, marches and pretty duets, written especially for the mandolin. They practised, over months and months, to attain a reasonable standard of playing technique and it all sounded beautiful. John taught me the mandolin and right from the word go I wanted, eventually, to get a guitar so that I could sing and accompany myself at the same time. My cousins, Paddy and Derry Kavanagh, with my pal, Mickey Brennan, all loved to get together with me when we would do some 'head' (impromptu) arrangements of current songs, then we'd all sing in harmony à la the Mills Brothers or the Sons of the Pioneers.

My great love was going to the film matinées on Saturday afternoons where, for the princely sum of four old pence, we'd get two and a half hours of our heroes in action. Since, I suppose, I had from the start a sneaking regard for the singing cowboys – such as Roy Rogers and Gene Autry – they held a special place in my roll of honour as far as entertainment went. I'd sit in the gods, feet on the wooden bench and bottoms perched painfully on the backrest, indifferent to the fact that two hours of it entailed a most uncomfortable walk home in the late afternoon.

It's quite exciting to remember that I'd listen to Rogers or Autry sing their latest songs, then take home enough of a mental recording to enable me to sing them later on and, in fact, dictate the harmony to my own harmony group. I'm sure that all this early training could be one of the reasons I find it possible, these days, to memorise my weekly television shows when called upon to do them live.

I was in the States recently and watched some of those old western movies and, I must say, they still had a great nostalgic effect on me. I wrote a fan letter to Gene Autry when I was about seven years old but I didn't get the requested photograph for which I waited months. Mind you, the chances are that I sent the letter to Gene Autry, Cowboy, America – so what could I expect? Imagine my feelings, many years later, when I was honoured to be the subject of *This Is Your Life* to find, as one of my guests, Mr Autry himself offering his good wishes and a sincere apology for not answering my letter!

My parents were very careful not to have their domestic tiffs in front of us and usually waited until they were alone. At least, I'm assuming they had them in our absence as they certainly refrained from rowing in our presence.

One evening, when I was still very young, I was up in bed huddled-up in my blankets and hugging a rolled-up piece of cloth inside which my mother had put a heated flat-iron. This was my hotwater bottle, which had been placed by the side of the fire throughout the evening, building up a terrific heat, then at bedtime popped between the blankets so that the heat lasted well into the night. Anyway, on this particular night, the sound of voices raised in anger carried up into my room, making me pull the blankets from around my face so that I could listen. Lying on my back I could hear more clearly and discovered that the subject of the confrontation was, in fact, myself.

You see, I had no decent shoes to wear to school and my mother was telling my father that she could not afford them from the money she was being given, so she thought my father's conscience should force him to do something about it. Finally, I heard him bring the matter to a close.

'OK, that's enough, woman, leave it at that. You get the boy to meet me tomorrow outside "the job" and I'll get him some shoes.'

Tomorrow being Saturday, my father finished work at 12.30 and, on my mother's instructions, I was stationed very firmly by the outside gate. The knock-off whistle

went at 12.30, sounding a bit like the 'All Clear' signal.
Scores of men of all shapes, ages and sizes, descended on
the entrance yard and approached the main-gates like a
crowd of football supporters leaving the ground.

My eyes darted anxiously from man to man, trying to
locate the familiar figure of my dad and, just as I was
about to think I'd missed him, there he was walking
towards me, smiling.

'Are we all set then, boy, eh? Well, let's get those shoes.'
He put his hand on my shoulder and off we went, heading
for the town centre.

We'd only gone a few hundred yards, when he said:
'Hang on there a minute, son. I won't be long,' and
disappeared through the door of one of his favourite pubs.
I sat on the kerb outside, worrying that the shops might be
closed before he came out. Eventually, he re-appeared
adjusting his moustache and looking determined to head
straight for the shoe shop ... it wasn't to be!

His next call, was his favourite second-hand book shop
where, as I've mentioned earlier, he would stock-up for his
week's reading. He fished about among all the grubby
looking publications – picking them up, flicking through
them, asking the odd question then, finally, made a
choice. It was now nearing 1.30 – and I was no nearer to
being shod.

Well, finally, we walked through the doors of one of the
town's finest shoeshops. The heavy leathery smell hit my
nose like a punch from a boxing glove. That smell,
coupled with the darkness of the place and the fact that it
was alive with busy shoppers and their families, all
smelling of cows, pigs and damp clothes from the light
drizzle outside, made this, one of my rare visits to such an
establishment, a disappointment.

My father approached the shop assistant, 'Good day to
ya',' he said, in a way that suggested the lad should ignore
all his other waiting customers and attend to me – and I
was half hoping he wouldn't.

I heard my father's voice above the chatter: 'Yes, yes, you

give this lad a good pair of shoes and look after him well, I'll be back in time to pay for them.' He then motioned me to a leather-backed chair against the wall and said, 'This man will see to you, boy. I'll be back in a few minutes.' I patiently awaited my turn and it must have been a long wait because, when the man came to attend to my needs, the shop had practically emptied.

'Now then, young fella,' he began, 'what can we do for you?' I must have looked a bit blank, because he simply paused for a few seconds and then went on, 'What would you like, boots or shoes?'

I said I really didn't mind but that my mother had told me to get something smart and strong enough to last a long time.

'I see,' he said. 'Brown or black?'

'I don't mind,' I said again.

He went up his little ladder and began to pull down all sorts of boxes. Out came brown shoes, black boots, brown boots, black shoes, ones with tips on the heels, with toe-caps, without toe-caps, ones with a little loop at the back that you put your finger through to pull the thing over the heel.

When I was finally fitted-out with my lovely new footwear, he slapped me on the knee and said, 'Well now, how is that?'

I said it was grand and sat there in my seat, wondering what the hell to do next. Where was my father to pay for them?

I continued to sit on that chair. The shop was completely deserted; every now and then somebody would come in, look at me, look at my shoes, make some enquiry about the price of an article in the window and then leave. The boss and his staff stood behind the counter, the men drinking mugs of tea and the boss himself holding a glass containing something a bit more interesting. I wanted to go to the door to look out for any sign of my father but was afraid that the boss would think I was trying to make a run for it. I felt awful, thinking that all the whispering behind the counter was probably about me. I even thought of taking off my new shoes, quietly slipping out of the shop, and heading for home which was about a mile away. The street outside was still very busy with horses and carts, motor cars, lorries; all their sounds mingling with those of the cattle being herded into carts to be transported back into the country.

At last, I could bear the strain no longer. Seeing that the time, by the old clock on the shop wall, was 2.45 p.m. I stood up and walked painfully towards the door, where I stood gazing at the entrance to the pub across the road. At the same moment, as if by some miracle, the door of the pub opened and out walked three men – the last one was my father. They all started to bid each other those fond farewells that only boozing pals indulge in: slapping each other's shoulders and behaving as if each one was emigrating to a different foreign part and, beyond any doubt, they would never meet again.

My father gave a final flourish of farewells, looked towards the shoeshop and made a bee-line in my direction. My feelings of joy turned to horror as he walked, quite casually, into the path of an oncoming car. There was a screech of brakes – and then, screaming and panic from the onlookers!

Now, I don't know what your reaction would be in such a situation and I don't know why mine was – as it turned out to be. I didn't run to my father's side, I didn't stop to find out if he was OK, my only thought was that I couldn't face those men in the shop again when my father looked as though he was in no fit state to pay for the shoes. I simply took a deep breath and ran like hell for a mile to my home. New shoes. Well, I dread to think how my poor feet felt about the whole thing – I'm sure they've never forgiven me. I went through the house like a tornado, to find my mother standing over a big tin bath dipping the sheets she'd washed in blue.

She looked at me, standing there, panting, 'Oh! you've got the shoes, good boy. They look grand.'

I gulped, 'Daddy's been run over by car – and he might be dead!'

My mother looked up and smiled, 'It would take more than a car to kill your father, boy,' she said, drying her hands on her apron. 'Come on, you just sit down and have your dinner. You must be starving.'

I don't know what I thought at that moment, but, I do know, that father came in about half an hour later, with a plaster on his face. He had paid for the shoes and all was well ... He sat down and had his dinner too!

3 The Three-and-Sixpenny Bicycle

In view of the constant publicity given to the religious conflict in Ireland, I've often asked myself if I recall from my childhood any feelings of bigotry towards those of a different persuasion from my own. I have to admit that, in all honesty, my only assessment of the non-Catholic members of the community was that we didn't know them very well and they were usually better off than we were. They had better houses and were often members of the golf or tennis clubs but I don't think there was any resentment between us although, of course, Catholic and non-Catholic children were educated separately.

School for me, on the whole, was good. I suppose I was about average from the IQ point of view but then, we didn't talk about IQ in my youth or, at least, if it was talked about, I didn't notice. I went to the National School which was looked after by the De La Salle Brothers, and a good hard healthy schooling it was too. You worked hard or got a clip round the ear and we never questioned the authority of the teachers; when we got out into the playground we called them all sorts of names but, in the classroom, we toed the line.

My education actually began at the Convent School, when I was about four years old. My brother Lar took me on my first day and, very shyly, I sat down in a classroom of little boys and girls, all writing on slates with pieces of chalk. It was in fact a girl's school, but they were kind enough to accept some of the little lads as kindergarten pupils to keep them out of harm's way. I loved it when the Nun said it was time to go home; she was a big, red-faced lady who smelled of soap. However, I don't think I was long there before I went to St Declan's National School for boys.

I was fairly well behaved then and never much good at breaking the rules – I always felt it was too much trouble coping with the intrigue. One of my pals rarely did his 'ecker' but would meet me every morning and copy mine word for word. When we got into class the teacher would walk around the room checking-up on us. He'd take a look at my work book, tick off the rights and wrongs, make some appropriate remark then, turn to my pal and say, 'I suppose yours is the same.' And pass on to the next desk. I honestly think he'd given that fellow up as a bad job and just hoped he'd win the pools, or something.

I always did well at exams in those early days, usually finishing near the top of my class each year. My favourite subjects were art, music and maths. (It hasn't lasted with maths though: I can't be bothered with money matters at all and really do look upon it as a 'necessary evil'. Everybody tells me this attitude is typical of a fellow who's not short of a few bob, maybe they're right!) I played hurling, football (Gaelic, that is), handball, was in the school's gym team and, to use a present day show-business term, was 'middle of the road' at all of them.

We had a super school choir at St Declans and won all sorts of acclaim for our harmony singing. I was in the bottom section and only last year renewed the acquaintance of our old choir master from those great days. I'm glad he didn't say, 'I always knew you'd do well at the singing, son.' I hate to hear a man of the cloth tell lies!

Only once in my whole school life did I 'mitch' (that's the Waterford term for playing truant). Even then, I didn't just not go to school. I went, sat in the classroom and, at the right moment, approached the Brother's table.

He looked up, '*Bhail, a Mhicil, ar mhait leat dul amach?*' ('Well, Michael' – which is my first name, as I have already said – 'would you like to leave the room?')

I then told him, in Irish, that my mother had to go to work and wanted me to do some things at home.

He trusted me implicitly and said, '*Tá go maith abaile leat anois agus bí annso maidean am aireach.*' (OK, off with you and be here tomorrow morning.)

I never realised that being a crook could be so easy and I gave him a sad look, which could only be that of a lad whose mother had to go out to work and he has to do all sorts of things at home. I knew that my pal, who hadn't come to school at all, would be waiting in the park across the road, so off I went.

Galloping down the steps to the street, I dashed through the gates and straight into the arms of my mother – who happened to be passing at the time. I realised, from that moment, that I'd never make it in a life of crime.

'Where are you off to?' asked mother.

'Ah! nowhere ... I'm doing something for the Brother,' I stuttered.

'Well, hurry up then and get back to school,' she said and pulled her coat around her, as she walked off towards the shops.

I hung around for a bit and then, having given things some thought, slunk back into school. The teacher was pleased things had picked-up for the family – and the matter was closed.

Not surprisingly, when later on I went into the secondary school, which was run by the same Order of Brothers and called De La Salle College, and things *did* become a bit difficult at home, my academic standard took a turn for the worse and pretty soon I was way down in the list of runners when exam time came round.

At the Convent School across the road from our house, the nuns used to cater for certain children at lunch time by giving them a small half-pint bottle of milk and a currant bun with a sugary top. Invariably, when the lunch break was over and the crates of empty milk bottles put away in the school outhouse adjoining the robery (or cloakroom), one or two currant buns also returned with the leftovers. I and my fellow vultures often hung about our old school and 'cased the joint'. If we saw that the rock-bun situation was worth pursuing, we'd have a planning meeting.

Sometimes we would slip into the shed and eat them in there – while giving some stick to a packet of five Woodbines – other times we'd simply nick the buns, take them back to our den and eat them in comfort.

One day we went into the shed, lit our fags and began to eat our buns, when we heard the swish-swishing sound of an approaching Nun. The Sisters wore black habits and around their waists they'd have long Rosary beads which hung down at one side. They also had a black leather strap hanging side by side with the Rosary so, when an angry hand shot to the hip, you never quite knew whether you were going to be belted or prayed for. The swishing movement reached the door of the outhouse and somebody stopped outside. We sat quietly in the corner waving our hands about to disperse the smoke. We heard a key in the door, the lock clicking home and then, to our horror, the swishing skirts slowly fading into the distance – we were locked in!

Well, we sat there and ate the buns, wondering if we'd ever see our families again. Time seemed endless and darkness began to change the whole childish prank into a bit of a nightmare. Much later, we heard the faint sound of a woman's voice coming from the direction of the school and peeping through the window saw a Sister approaching, carrying an empty coal scuttle. With mixed feelings of being caught and rescued at the same time, we stood back against the wall in the dark corner trying to look inconspicuous. The Nun opened the door, laid down the coal scuttle on the floor then, in the light of the open doorway, we saw her fingering through the keys as she continued her gentle song. She selected a key and turned on her heel, heading for the door of the adjoining robery. We heard the cloakroom door open, the song went down a notch in volume indicating that she'd gone through the door, and then we made our move. In seconds, we were through the playground and down the street.

A couple of hours later I was sitting at home, when a great commotion outside caused the entire household to rush into the street. Somebody was shouting, 'Call the fire brigade,' and reporting that smoke was coming from the shed next to the cloakroom at the school. No damage was done however and the mini-fire was soon extinguished.

I heard somebody say, 'They found cigarette butts in there.'

My father retorted, 'The Nuns smoking? A likely story!'

In winter, there was a big coal fire at the top of our classroom at St Declan's, with a long black firescreen around it. Even though the room was still cold at the opposite end the look of the fire was always welcome. It was absolute heaven to stand by it for a minute, especially if you'd just gone through the rigours of visiting the outside toilets. Strangely enough, one of the few unhappy memories of my boyhood was that of feeling cold. I hated the cold when I was a kid and wished for the biggest of fires at all times. Mind you, the old houses were cold and damp and I'm sure they carried the chill of many winters in their plaster walls. I can still hear my mother's repeated warning: 'Go easy on that coal, boy! We haven't got much and it's gone up again!' We learned to relish every spark of its lovely heat – so much so, in fact, that even today I hate to go to bed at night and leave a nice fire burning in the grate. I feel it's such a sin to lie in my warm bed, while all that warmth is wasting away downstairs. Like my wife, I've always felt that I'd rather be warm and hungry than have ample food and be cold.

Special treats in those days came in the form of something tasty for tea, going to a local concert, or getting something new to wear. It really is a shame, as I often express in songs I sing on television, that these simple pleasures have become mundane and ordinary things.

Our bread used to be delivered by a man with a horse and a rather fancy cart with the baker's name on the side – in time, of course, it was brought to us in a van. One of the greatest thrills of my life came when the breadman allowed me to join him on his rounds, carrying a basket from the van to the different front doors.

One great day he said he had to make a special delivery to a place called Dunmore East – a very pretty fishing village some seven or so miles from my home. On the day in question I was overjoyed to find that the local regatta was on there. It was a beautiful day: the harbour filled with boats, bunting strewn over the fishing fleet and people in happy holiday moods. The breadman went about his deliveries and I sat on the rocks watching the boat races and the greasy-pole competition, while music poured from the loudspeaker perched high on the telegraph poles. It was magical. Too magical, in fact. I was so carried away by the excitement of it all that I forgot to do as I'd promised and ask somebody the time to make sure that I joined my kind delivery man at a prearranged time and place.

Well, we lost each other and there I was, seven miles from home, tired and hungry, with no money and no way of getting back. All excitement gone and feeling miserable and frightened, I began to make my way towards the road leading to town. The cars were few and far between, the pony and traps only concerned with the local passengers, so hope of a lift faded as I walked up the hill from this beautiful little place. By the time I'd walked some two or three miles, I was exhausted and absolutely starving.

I'll never forget reaching the stage when I was forced to go up to a cottage, knock on the door and ask for something to eat and drink. Knowing, only too well, how kind and hospitable my fellow countrymen are, I still can't believe what happened.

A crusty old lady opened the door.

'Ah! please could I have a piece of bread and jam and a cup of water?' I asked. (You can almost hear the 'hearts and flowers' can't you?)

The old lady looked at me for a second or two then, waving the back of her hand towards me, she shouted, 'Be off with ya, ya cheeky little divil, and get home to yer mother!'

She banged the door and I went down the path with my tail between my weary legs and I'm sure that that lady never realised then that she would go down in my book as the most horrible old witch I'd ever met. I got home some hours later and the breadman had told my mother what had happened. My feet are getting better though!

Making my own recreation was almost an obsession with me from an early age but, sadly, boredom seems to be a sort of password among many young people today. They blame boredom for all kinds of things that they do and shouldn't do, or things that they should do, but won't. Maybe I was lucky but, as a boy, I spent hours and hours doing the most simple and naïve things with my spare time.

'I'm going to make my own comic book,' I told my dad one evening.

'Good for you, boy,' he said. 'And I hope it sells be the thousand.'

Needless to say, I had my personal supply of copies of *Hotspur, Champion,* not to mention *Beano* and *Dandy,* tucked away under my little fireside stool. I used these as my guide.

First I had to find a name for it and plumped for 'The Valiant', because it sounded like my own name. I created my characters, drew them, made up my little story lines and then set about doing the actual comic strips. I wrote a short adventure story for the centre pages and even threw in a couple of puzzles and games for good measure. The whole thing looked great to me when I'd finished colouring the pictures; although I hadn't dreamed that there would be so much work involved. Proudly I passed it on to my pals, who thought it was quite good. The idea even became infectious and pretty soon there were quite a few home-made comics round the place. At Christmas time I would try to make gifts for my friends and worked hard at making special cards. I still make the cards to this day – on birthdays and other special occasions which are being celebrated by those I love.

Speaking of Christmas reminds me of a rather special festive presentation I was involved in at school when I was about six years old. As it was to be performed in front of our families and friends I found the whole thing very exciting, if a bit nerve-wracking. I became a member of a little orchestra which was to feature home-made instruments of the most weird and wonderful varieties. The 'front-line', or melody section, consisted mainly of comb and paper players – a part of the orchestra I was hoping I could avoid, since I've never been able to stand the way this particular instrument tickled my lips. Thank goodness I was booked into the rhythm section which included the strangest concoction of 'clanging', 'banging', 'scraping' and 'pinging' noises you've ever heard.

Another young fellow and myself were to make up the section known as 'The Jamjargonettes'. There we stood, a two-pound jamjar hanging by a string from our left hands, looking for all the world as if we'd lost our tiddlers. In our right hands we held a six-inch nail partly covered with tape in case we stabbed ourselves to death or broke our jamjars during a crescendo! On a given cue we would beat out the time by banging the six-inch nail against the jar, at the same time singing in unison with the rest of the orchestra:

> Oh! we are the Emergency Band
> Yes, we are the Emergency Band
> We can sing
> We can dance
> We can laugh
> We can PRAAAANCE!!
> We are the Emergency Band
> PING PING! PING!

As we pinged our way through the first week's rehearsal, little did I know that my first acting role was on the horizon. At one stage the conductor turned to us to say, 'Are we all present?' to which we answered, 'But, of course!' He then called each section in turn and when he said, 'Jamjargonettes?' I had to point the six-inch nail at

44

my chest and say, 'Do you refer to us?' My mother made me a special uniform for the occasion: green silk trousers and a yellow blouse. I practised my pings and my special line so much, that as my family sat there on opening night and I said, 'Do you refer to us?' they actually applauded. It was all a bit too much for me, I think, because I let my six-inch nail fall to the floor. It went down between the floorboards and I had to finish the concert with my finger. Well, it was an 'Emergency Band', after all!

Living within a few miles of the sea, we had the good fortune to be within easy reach of natural beaches which were part and parcel of our very attractive coastline. My favourite was a little place called Woodstown – not the kind of spot you think of as a seaside resort. Indeed, there was no town at all, no hotels and no houses to speak of either, there was simply a very unsophisticated beach stretching for about a couple of miles separated from the road by a raised terrace of sandhills. These were an absolute maze of little humps and hollows which, at weekends, were snapped up by eager families as their private nests for the day. Each little hideaway served as a changing-room, dining-room, nursery or love nest, depending on the relationship of the occupants.

We spent hundreds of idyllic days at this charming spot, getting there either on foot, bicycle or, on very privileged occasions, by car. My father knew a man who had a car-hire firm and, by some means or other, managed to treat us to that very special day out in a car. The car, on reflection, looked like the ones used by Al Capone or Bonnie and Clyde. But Woodstown became a second home to me and my pals, once I finally managed to acquire my own bicycle – which came about in a strange way.

A couple of miles from my home, at a place called Grantstown, there was an old country house, the grounds of which were used as playing fields for a private school in Waterford. The pupils from the Bishop Foy School came there several afternoons a week to play rugby, hockey or cricket. At the entrance to the premises there was a very small gatehouse in which lived a family named Brennan. Old Mr Brennan was a retired school teacher and my rather vague memory of him is that he looked like George Bernard Shaw and could often be seen, on summer afternoons, sitting on the wall outside the main gate quietly playing a bamboo pipe which he'd fashioned himself. His daughter, affectionately known as Babby, ran a minute confectioner's shop inside the house – one purpose of which was to supply the schoolboys with light refreshments and cigarettes.

My father was very friendly with the Brennan family and always popped in there during his country walks. This pleased me no end as it meant a nice slice of home-made cake and a bottle of lemonade. In return for this special treat, I'd walk 400 yards down the road to the nearby well and fill a big enamel bucket with water for use in the Brennan household. This, as you'll conclude, did not have running water. On other occasions I'd break up a week's supply of kindling for their fire or go out into their back garden and collect a basket of eggs from the hen-houses.

When old Mr Brennan died I would, on the instructions of my father, make frequent after-school visits to Grantstown to help them cope with extra chores. It was a labour of love since I enjoyed being in the country and also loved to sit in the long grass and watch the boys playing cricket or hockey; games never played at the National Schools.

You had to keep a sharp watch out at about four o'clock when the boys arrived because they usually came careering down the hill on their bikes and turned sharply through the gate at a dangerous speed. Babby constantly asked them to slow down as she feared the worst would happen if ever their arrival coincided with some local person leaving the shop.

All her pleading was in vain so, in time, the solution was arrived at by the local Guards (Irish Police) who suggested that the gates be kept closed. This forced the boys to dismount at the entrance, wheel their bicycles through the gates, then remount to go to the pavilion. I never knew that this new ruling was to bring me good fortune!

One of the boys came down the hill one day, turned the corner into the entrance – the gate was closed, and he just couldn't stop in time. The result was a very buckled front wheel and a very bruised young man. Some minor first-aid treatment was administered and the wrecked bike left in the garden shed for safe keeping.

After a couple of weeks the same lad arrived on a brand new bicycle and, from then on, I spent many hours gazing enviously at the old rusting model with the damaged wheel lying in the outhouse.

I asked Babby what the chances would be of my acquiring it knowing, in my heart, that if it cost even one pound, it would be out of the question. When she felt that the time was right she popped the question which, luckily for me, came on the same day as her request for his account to be settled. His reaction suggested that he had forgotten the old 'crock' and without hesitation he said, 'Let him pay my bill and he can have it!' He owed three shillings and sixpence.

I chose my moment carefully and put the proposition to my father.

'How much?' he asked.

'Three and six.'

'What kind of a bike is that?'

I assured him that it was beautiful.

'I'll look at it on Sunday,' he said, 'then we'll see!'

The rest of the week just crawled by but, on Sunday, when I proudly opened the shed for my dad and lifted the bike into a standing position, he examined the wheel, then the slightly bent handlebars and with a grunt of amusement said, 'That's a grand little thing. I'll pay for it, and you get it home.'

That afternoon I rolled my newly acquired treasure, on

47

the back wheel only, along the mile or two of road to my home. My family admired it and made me feel thoroughly proud of my first business deal. My dad had me take it to a local shop, where the repairs were done in a couple of days: the handlebars were fixed and a second-hand wheel replaced the damaged one. By the following weekend, after several days of oiling, cleaning, painting and polishing, I was the owner of what was to be one of the most exciting things I've ever had. As I said, from that day on, Woodstown became my second home.

One day, when the tide was full in, I went swimming with the boys and, some couple of hours later as the tide had gone a long way out, we decided to pick some cockles for our families to eat. I had a huge bag of them as I trundled up the beach and then, to my absolute horror, I found my bicycle had gone! I sat down in total dejection, feeling as though my world had come to an end. The lads, whose bikes were OK, offered me a lift home on the crossbar of one of their machines. The evening shadows made the countryside look dull and wintery as we set off for home and, suddenly, I didn't want to go.

'You go on,' I said, 'I'll have another look for my bike. Tell my mother I'm OK.' And, all alone, I headed back to the deserted sandhills.

I walked up and down hope fading more and more with each trip when, across the dunes, I heard my name being called. I ran to the road to find one of my pals approaching, pushing his bike.

'We've found it,' he said. 'It's just thrown in the ditch down the road. Whoever took it just had a ride, then threw it away.'

With a feeling of sheer joy surging up in my throat, I ran through the semi-darkness to the spot where my dear old companion was lying on its side. I felt so happy that, as my father would say, 'I wouldn't call the Queen me Aunt.'

Off we went and before we were half way home it was pitch dark but we knew the road so well that the darkness didn't bother us as we chatted to each other. We saw a light approaching, it was a Guard.

'Where's your lamps?' he said, and there followed a long story about the cockles, the stolen bicycle, etc.

'What's your name?' the guard asked.

'Val Doonican,' I said.

'Are you Johnny Doonican's young fella?' he asked me.

'Yes,' I answered.

He put his hand in his pocket and took out a torch. 'Here,' he said, 'take this and be on your way. I'll call and collect it in the morning.'

What a lovely day that was; the cockles, by the way, were delicious!

About a quarter of a mile from our house, at the top of a little country road we christened Looby Lane, a very large field had been apportioned into several allotments, or 'plots' as we preferred to call them. Dad managed to get one or, should I say, the use of one, and promptly laid it out into neat rows of potatoes, carrots, cabbages, onions, and as many other domestic vegetables as its limited space could accommodate. Most evenings, if the weather was agreeable, he'd wander up there, keeping a close eye on the progress of his crop, weeding a bit here, thinning out a bit there. I loved to go with him and soon learned how to plant the various things and also got to know when they were ready for the kitchen.

When the time came for Dad and I to harvest the potatoes, I was always fascinated by the very smallest of the crop which lay sprinkled about the drills like tiny marbles.

'Pick those up, boy,' my dad would say. 'Put them in a separate bag and hang on to them.'

When we got back home I'd pop my bag of miniature spuds behind the gas stove in the kitchen and forget about them. Then, maybe some nights later when my mother would be gone out to visit a relative or friend, he'd put down his book, wink at me and head for the kitchen door.

Half an hour later we'd sit by the fireside sharing a plateful of the little floury morsels sprinkled with salt and dipped in butter, thinking about all the people who were silly enough to throw this veritable treat on the compost heap with their weeds. They didn't know what they were missing.

The most popular seaside spot in the area was undoubtedly Tramore, some six or seven miles from Waterford. We cycled there quite regularly and enjoyed the facilities it proudly offered to the thousands who flocked there throughout the summer. Its magnificent golden beach stretched for miles, from the little town itself to the far off sandhills behind which lay our precious Woodstown. Mind you, to us children Tramore took on the dimensions of a miniature Blackpool. It was the only place in the area which possessed such exotic attractions as a funfare, amusement arcades, dance halls and a long promenade where you could take a stroll and, at the same time, watch the teaming masses enjoying themselves on the sands below.

For me, Tramore's *pièce de résistance* was its unique railway system: a single line service which ran from a tiny station in Waterford right to the edge of the sea. So convenient in fact, that you simply stepped off the train and in a moment or two were settled with your family on the beach. I was indeed saddened, some twenty years back, when told by my family that the Tramore Railway had closed down and was no more. The magical memories of those little carriages, smelling of burning coal, being trundled along by that big old-fashioned engine, belching out its plumes of black smoke, are still such precious things to me.

'Keep that window shut,' my mother would say. 'You'll get a spark in your eye, then we'll hear all about it!' Our buckets and spades would be stacked on the racks above, while my mother held the carrier-bag loaded with sandwiches, drinks and, of course, our swimming things. It was like going to Miami Beach for a month as far as we were concerned and, time after time, I stood face pressed to the window counting the 'tunnels' as we called them. They were merely tiny bridges, facilitating the country roads criss-crossing the line from time to time, but they became our way of determining how much longer we would have to wait before reaching the station and setting off for the sea.

The Tramore Train
Going to the seaside in the early 1930s

One momentous day the Tramore train didn't stop at the station – it went straight on, through the buffers, through the end of the building and out on to the road leading to the seafront! It was the most wonderful piece of drama, giving us all sorts of thrills, causing all sorts of questions to be asked – not least of them being, 'How the hell do we get home?' Any time I sit and watch films about the old days on the railways of the past, I can't help going back in my thoughts to those beautiful times of the Tramore Train.

Watching the boys from Bishop Foy's School at their games gave me a yen to have a go at playing cricket. I'd never had a proper cricket bat in my hand and, strangely enough, I still haven't! In the centre of the road, just outside our front door, there was a large circular manhole. It was a spot I avoided since my father had instructed me, very early on, not to indulge in my habit of trying to peep through the grating to see if there was water flowing at the bottom of the hole. 'You'll inhale the germs,' he warned. However, the thing turned out to have a good use.

Dad made a set of wooden cricket stumps which fitted neatly into the apertures in the manhole cover, so, with a tennis ball and a hurley, we were set for our local test match. There was one rather large slit in the cover of the manhole and this, we decided, would be the crease. One day one of my pals who was batting at the crease hit a beautiful six into the grounds of the county hospital and, in so doing, brought our game to an unexpected end. They said the grounds were out of bounds for us kids. After much discussion we decided to finish our game using a sliothar (the ball used for the game of hurling). It's made of cowhide and is formed something like a tennis ball – the two pieces stitched together with Wax-end. This ball is very hard and should be treated with respect.

Anyway, our fast bowler came thundering in and let the ball fly at the stumps. The batsman made a full-blooded swipe at it and the ball caught him clean on the knuckles. He let out a wild scream and let go of the hurley which slipped gently through the 'crease' and went sailing through space to the bottom of the manhole some fifteen feet below the road. Everything went silent as the batsman recovered his composure and came to terms with the fact that first he had lost my tennis ball and now my hurley. He went through the motions of apologising, knowing it would never undo the dreadful damage he had done. We all stared at him for a bit and then, the boss of our gang spoke:

'You'll have to go down and get it,' he said. 'And then you'll have to climb the hospital wall and get the tennis ball.'

It took four of us to lift the three-inch thick cover off the top of the manhole, and peering down into the bowels of the earth we could see about a dozen little metal rungs attached to the wall, especially put there for the rare descents into this forbidding place. Shaking with fear, our poor victim began to disappear into the darkness. His head had just dipped below ground level when one of the group, holding the cover up on its side, suddenly shouted, 'Here comes Val's father!' The manhole top plopped back into its original position and six guilty looking legs disappeared in different directions.

My father approached the house and shouted hello to me as I stood innocently against the lamp-post. 'Coming in for tea?' he asked. I hesitated for a moment and then thought I'd better show willing. My mother was serving up the meal and I knew there was no possible way I could sit and eat it while my poor playmate was buried in a smelly manhole, not knowing when he would be released from his misery.

I found some excuse to pop outside for a minute and was so relieved to find a group of lads kneeling round the open manhole and a very pale and frightened boy emerging into the light of day once again.

I felt very guilty about that incident and I went round the next day and gave the young fella a book that I'd been given – as a sort of peace offering.

As in most localities, we had a tightly knit group of young lads who made up our little 'gang'. As ever, the leader was the one with the most dominant personality. Our particular 'Yul Brynner' wielded enormous power over his Magnificent Seven: deciding what games we would play, where we would go, and who was going to participate in whatever activities he'd chosen.

In addition to his qualities of leadership, he had a great advantage in being the proud owner of a little outhouse adjoining his home, where we could meet when the weather was unfavourable.

We played all the usual games, of course, including Cowboys and Indians. The casting was done by our leader, and depending on how you stood in his favours, you could find yourself playing such a plum role as sheriff or marshall, or, on the other hand, you could be shot in the first reel.

One of our favourite places for outdoor games was an area of rugged countryside nearby, known as The Knock. We went there one afternoon to act out some great western adventure and, as the various roles were being allocated, one of the less favoured pals on that day arrived, hoping to be included.

'Scratchy', as he was called, hung about like an out-of-work actor, hoping that the Magnificent Seven, might for some reason or another find themselves reduced to six. When all the parts were filled, 'Yul Brynner' must have felt a slight twinge of guilt, so he turned to 'Scratchy'.

'Tell you what,' he said. 'You can be the lookout, OK?'

'What do I have to do?' said the eager Scratchy.

'Take your gun, go up to the top of the hill and sit on the rock. Just watch the road down through the fields, and let us know if you see any of the bad fellas comin', OK?'

Scratchy climbed to the lookout post on top of the rock and sat in the sun, his gun at the ready.

The main action was just getting under way amongst the rocks, when a little kid came running from the woods and shouted to our leader: 'Hey, yer mammy says yer to come home, take the "truck" (handcart) and get a half-hundred of coal.'

The action stopped, 'Aw bugger it,' says 'Yul Brynner', putting his gun in its holster. He gave us one of those 'follow-me-men' waves and we all headed for town – all of us, that is, except for poor Scratchy, who was still on duty on the rocks overlooking the fields, and unaware that the film was over. He might still be there for all I know. Such is the life of the supporting actor.

4 Looby Lane

When I was about thirteen my father began to do some strange things, to my way of thinking. I'd see him at home at times when he would normally be working then, for some peculiar reason, he would go away to Wales or England or somewhere – I can't recall for how long but, when he came back, he seemed to come in and out of the house all the time dressed in his best blue serge suit and his bowler hat. Then I heard my mother mention that he had sold his precious box of tools; something very odd was going on at home and I didn't know what it was. What I didn't know, in fact, was that my father was ill.

One day he called me into the hut and confided that he wanted me to do something special for him. 'Now then,' he said, sitting on the edge of his bed, 'there's no need to let your mother know anything about this, OK?' This, I remember, struck me as being very odd, as it had always been quite impossible to keep any secrets in our small and crowded home. Anyway I agreed and awaited my instructions, which he gave me as follows: 'Now, you know Looby Lane' (a little country lane, near our home, which was very overgrown with bushes and nettles and used only by people walking their dogs or courting couples), 'well, if you walk up there, you'll find the blackberry briars are just coming into blossom. You'll see lots of little pale green buds on each briar. Now, take this jamjar and scissors, cut the briars off about two inches long and bring them back to me, OK? Remember now, mum's-the-word!'

I was puzzled, to put it mildly; keeping the cutting of blackberry briars secret from my mother was quite beyond me. However, I took my James Bond style task and went sneaking through the house, carrying my jamjar, while my mom was too busy to notice. A short while later, I sneaked into the hut and passed over the goods to my father.

I plucked up courage before I left and asked, 'What are they for?'

He looked up at me, put his finger to his lips and said, 'Remember, mum's-the-word!'

I then forgot the matter, for the rest of the evening.

As I've mentioned, our only running water was a tap on the wall in our backyard and this was where I had my morning wash before going to school – at least, during the mild weather. When I was going out to wash my face the day after the 'blackberry job', my mother called out to me to empty some rubbish into the dustbin. When I lifted the lid off our rubbish bin, I was greeted with the sight of a bunch of something green and wet lying at the bottom – on closer inspection I found it was the blackberry briars!

The incident was then forgotten as far as I was concerned, so you can imagine my feelings, some fifteen years later, while I was touring with a show in Scotland, when I found the answer. Back in my digs one evening, I was flicking through a very old book called *The Home Physician* when suddenly I saw 'Blackberry Briars'. I read on, 'It was widely believed in the country areas of Ireland, many years ago, that if you took the young buds from blackberry briars, boiled them and then drank the water it would cure ... cancer of the mouth and throat.'

When my father's illness became evident, even to me, I began to feel very sad because, even though very little in the way of real information came my way, I somehow felt that things were very serious. Indeed, it wasn't very long before my worst fears were confirmed and the news was broken to the whole family that he would have to go into hospital. He was, as far as I remember, about sixty-four years old when he left to spend his final days in the hospital, about ten minutes walk from our house. The cancer, with which he was stricken, started on his lip and it was possible to deduce from its location that it was caused, or at least aggravated, by the constant use of his old clay pipe.

I went to visit him every day after school and took him little presents from my mother such as tobacco, matches, newspapers and books. I'd sit on his bed and listen to him chat away about whatever happened to be on his mind. Sadly, as the days passed, his ramblings became more and more incomprehensible. One afternoon, when I was leaving the ward, the sister stopped me and began to ask me what I thought of him and if I liked coming to see him. I said that it upset me to find him in such obvious pain and she told me just how serious his condition was and appeared to be preparing me for the ensuing sadness.

The very next day, he appeared to have improved and talked to me in a perfectly normal and sane manner. When the time was up and I made signs of leaving, he took my hand and said, 'Now listen, boy.'

I slowly sank back on to the side of the bed and looked at him. By this time, by the way, the illness had distorted his face and mouth to such an extent that the hospital staff had bandaged his entire face and head, except for his eyes and nose which were still visible.

He continued, 'You know that I'm going to die, don't you?'

I nodded, 'Yes, mammy told me your sickness was serious.'

'Well,' he said, 'I think I will be going pretty soon, so I wanted to say something to you.' He paused and then went on, 'Now, you think I'm a great fella, don't you?'

'Yes, I do!' I answered without a second's hesitation.

'Before I go,' he went on, 'I think it's only fair that I should tell you that I'm not! You see, when I'm gone I know that in time people will say to you that your father was no good. Well, nothing would please me more than for you to say, "Yes, I know that, he told me himself".'

That is still the most wonderful thing I've ever known anybody do in my life: he made sure that the deep love I had for him could never be damaged.

It was only a few days after that final visit that my mother was told that my father had died; it came as a crushing blow to her, in spite of the fact that she had known it was only a matter of days. I chose not to go and see him at the hospital mortuary and, indeed, I said that I'd rather not attend the funeral either. When the day of the funeral arrived I explained, rather self-consciously, that I was going down to our local park to play football. All I really wanted to do was to escape from the house and everything that was, in any way, related to our tragic family situation.

I went to the park and took a football with me, but sitting under a tree feeling in no mood to play I looked around at the scene which brought so many memories of times in his company: the bandstand where we spent many evenings listening to our local brass and reed band giving their summer concerts; through the trees I could see 'the job' – the works where my father had spent the greater part of his life. I knew that, before long, at about three o'clock the funeral would come along the road which skirted the park. I was dreading this moment; so much so, that when I finally saw the slow moving procession of cars and the familiar figures of my brothers, Ned, John and Lar walking in line, I can actually remember standing up and hiding behind the tree. I waited until it had gone by and then, very slowly, made my way home to find my mother sitting by the fire having a cup of tea and being comforted by some of our very kind neighbours.

When my father had that final chat with me at the hospital, he confessed to not being a good husband to my mother and not being a very good father to us – and yet, even today, the deep impression he made on me is lasting evidence that his summing-up was far from accurate. My father gave me the most precious thing a parent can give, in my opinion, and that was his time and attention. I could not ask for any greater compliment than that my own children would remember me with a fraction of the same affection.

One of the most unique aspects of this story about my father, I might add, is that it's written by a man in his middle age using the memory of a fourteen-year-old boy. I have not researched his life through the eyes of any other member of the family and, consequently, have not been influenced in any way by conflicting opinions.

My father's passing left an incredible gap in our family life; my sisters Una and Nancy took over the running of the house to give Mom a respite, and somehow life took on a slightly different routine in this new set-up. However, jobs were hard to come by and money was scarce so my mother was forced to go out to work. She went, on certain days of the week, to a nearby house where she helped with various domestic chores. Payment for these services was a pittance but, in our circumstances, acted as a lifeline.

At a prearranged time I'd go to my mother's place of work and stand by the kitchen door till she came to the window and pass the money she'd earned out to me. I'd then hurry home, give it to my sister, who would run to the shops and so assure us of something for dinner. The lady for whom my mother worked was very kind and I can recall her coming into the yard behind the big house, leaving her horse in the care of a groom and then striding to the rear entrance of the house. She'd shout a hearty 'Hello' to me, ask me how I was and invariably offer me an apple. I'd accept gratefully and then go to the orchard nearby and take my pick.

Only a few years ago when I was visiting my mother in Ireland she mentioned that that same lady – who had become a good friend of hers – wanted more than anything to meet me. She was ninety years old, my mother informed me as we went to have lunch-time cocktails at her home by the sea, just outside Waterford. She remembered the apples and said she never failed to visualise me standing by the kitchen door, each time she watched my television shows.

By this time I'd reached secondary school status and daily attended the De La Salle College, some few minutes walk from the house. Just across the road from De La Salle College, was another educational establishment called Newtown School, whose name came from the road in which it stood. It was better known to us local people as 'The Quaker School', which is precisely what is was; the pupils came from all over the British Isles and the Continent. There was no contact between the two schools because we simply had nothing in common – even our games were different. The lads from the Quaker school played such sports as hockey, cricket and rugby, and we played the national ones like hurling, Gaelic football and handball. But we were always free to go to their sports fields and watch them play their various competitive sports, which we enjoyed very much.

At other times we would sit on top of the wall surrounding their playing fields and chant our disrespect for those who dared to be different from us, by singing:

> Proddy Proddy Bluebell
> never said his prayers.
> Catch him by the wooden leg
> and haul him down the stairs.
> The stairs gave a crack,
> Proddy broke his back
> and all the little ducks went
> 'Quack' 'Quack' 'Quack'.

Proddy, you'll no doubt conclude, was short for **Protestant** which to me, as a child, meant anyone who wasn't a Catholic. Why we should have sung our little ditty to Quakers, I'll never know. The difference between us children was, in fact, nothing more than that felt by supporters of two famous football teams. Mind you, that too can get out of hand to an alarming degree. As the De La Salle College was run by the same Brothers who had been responsible for my primary education at St Declan's, my change of schools simply meant, strictly speaking, just going to a different building.

The college was and still is a beautiful looking school,

built on top of a hill – it was always an imposing sight to my eyes.

The school clock, which is on a sort of mini-tower on top of the building, could be seen from many vantage points in the area, and became a very familiar landmark. When I see it today, I sometimes get a little shiver in my inside: memories of my final days there. They weren't too happy.

When I first went there, the headmaster – or superior – was a man named Brother Leo; a short, plump, bald-headed fellow with glasses.

For some reason, he was the only teacher I have ever had to whom I couldn't relate. Things, as I've said, were not too good at home and, even though I was allowed to buy my books on a weekly instalment basis (paying a mere shilling a week), I was constantly having to say that I just didn't have it. I should add, of course, that there were many other lads in exactly the same position.

Month by month, that morning trek to the classroom became more and more of a chore. Walking down Wilkin Street, which led from Passage Road to the school, I'd watch 'that clock' as it ominously approached our rather odd starting time of 9.10 am.

After about a year under Brother Leo's command the students were one day shocked to hear that he was to leave and take up a new post elsewhere. Some weeks later, he was gone.

The man who took his place was so different that he changed my whole attitude to school over those last couple of years. His name was Brother Bruno, a warm friendly man who went straight to the top of the charts as far as the lads were concerned – and stayed there. His reaction to my inability to pay for my books was to loan me some, either from the school library or from his own office.

He also became involved in the scouts and as, by now, I was a patrol leader, or something, I came in contact with him quite a lot. A great organiser, he had discipline worked out to a fine art. However, I'll tell you more about that later.

Our Latin Master was Brother Patrick, a great character who loved to join us in our sporting and scouting activities, cycle tours, camping holidays and country walks.

As I was beginning to find my academic life a bit heavy going, I was prone to daydreaming – especially during Latin. One morning my mind was miles away while 'Pakey', as we called him behind his back, rambled on about some paragraph in our text book *De Bello Gallico*. I was awakened from my dreaming by the sound of sniggering and, when I looked up, all eyes were in my direction.

Pakey broke the silence: 'Would you like to repeat what I've just said, Mr Doonican, in your own words of course – I doubt if mine made much impression on you.'

Slowly, I shuffled to my feet and, blushing to my hairline, mumbled, 'Ah, sorry, sir.'

Now Pakey had a funny way of shaking his head from side to side, while softly tut-tutting under his breath. When he finally ran out of shakes and tut-tuts, he gave me a very sad look, and spoke : 'Well, Mr Doonican, what are we going to do with you' ... tut-tut ... shake-shake ...'I don't know what you intend to do for a living, young man, but one thing I can assure you, mark my words, YOU WILL NOT DO IT VERY WELL.'

I've seen him in recent years and repeated his words. He did see the funny side of it.

Some time after I'd left school I was working in a band in the west of Ireland.

I went for a walk one day on a lonely country road to get some excercise before going out to work and I saw walking towards me a man in a black suit and clerical collar pushing his bicycle. The figure was unmistakable – it was Brother Leo; he'd been recently transferred to the local school nearby.

As we came face to face, I smiled a vague salutation,

wondering if he might remember me as one of his old boys. He slowed down as if to pass the time of day and rest his legs but didn't say anything much, he just sized me up.

'Hallo, Brother,' I said, knowing he was trying to put a name to the face.

Pointing a finger at me as if to say 'don't think you've got me fooled' he said, 'Kavanagh!'

This wasn't far out as it was my mother's name and the name of my cousins who went to the same school, and did resemble me in appearance.

Before I could reply, he shook his hand in front of my face.

'No! don't tell me,' he said. 'You're the other one. Doonican.' It was as if he'd won the jackpot.

'That's right,' I said, putting him out of his misery.

Well, we had a chat for a while, me feeling a little ashamed to tell him what I was doing for a living, as I felt sure he wouldn't approve. Some time later I heard the very sad news that he had been killed in a road accident.

Brother Bruno, in fact, left the De La Salle order shortly afterwards. He has been teaching at a college in Manchester for some years now; I've seen him on many occasions and had the pleasure of visiting him, his wife and family, at their Cheshire home.

We missed him a lot in the scouts, since he taught us everything from cooking to nature study and from first aid to tree felling. And he loved music: he'd organise the singsongs around the fire with the enthusiasm of a young lad, and joined in with everything. We had a pipe band in which I played first the tenor drums, swinging the sticks, with all kinds of well-rehearsed flourishes over my head as we paraded through the streets of my home town; later on, I was moved on to the bass drum, which was my instrument until the end of my scouting days. Playing the 'big drum' on a windy day can be a very hazardous occupation and one Sunday morning, in particular, proves my point.

We set out on what we called Mass Parade, a journey

63

that took us from our headquarters down a steep hill called Patrick Street, at the bottom of which we took a left turn into Bond Street and headed for the cathedral, near the quayside.

This Sunday was cold, blustery and not very inviting, especially for the members of the troop still wearing short trousers. (They didn't include me, by the way. I'd long given them up as my legs were not a pretty sight – even then.) Walking down Patrick Street wasn't too bad – it was quite a narrow thoroughfare, the buildings on both sides giving us shelter from the elements – but all the boys gritted their legs against the chill, as we began to round the corner at the bottom, knowing the wind was coming off the river and whipping up Broad Street. I'm not too sure how the gale-force wind did effect their poor knees but I can tell you how it affected me and my big drum. I was hit broadside by the blast of cold howling wind which, contrary to all my well-laid plans, sent me hurtling off at an angle of forty-five degrees – to the right. The rest of the band turned left!

I tried desperately to turn back and follow the boys but the wind repeated its fierce onslaught on the three-foot circular drumskin, which acted like a sail of a small dinghy, despatching me even further in the wrong dirction. Goodness knows where I would have finished up had it not been for the assistance of some passers-by, who grabbed hold of me and kept me from taking off completely. The boys had practically reached the cathedral by the time I rejoined them, ending a little episode that greatly amused both the boys and the many people standing watching along the pavements.

We also had 'Mass Parade'. when we went on our camping holidays each summer. The annual fortnight was spent at a beautiful seaside village called Stradbally, some twenty miles or so from Waterford. The camp-site was in a field, not more than a few hundred yards from a picturesque cove. The sea made the most lovely background to our little haven, and a river crossed the field just before ending its journey by joining the sea. This river was a perfect place for us lads to do our swimming, washing, fishing or just plain messing about. Across the road from where we spent our days was the entrance to a magnificent estate owned by Lord Waterford, who kindly allowed us not only to camp in his field but also to use his land for our general scouting activities – like rambling, nature study and tree felling. The latter was strictly supervised by the estate manager.

I went to do my tree-felling test one day, a particular tree having been designated for the event. Watched by one of my seniors I marked out my course of action on the tree then, picking up my sharpened axe, approached my 'victim' dressed only in shoes, socks and scouts shorts. Just as I was about to strike the first vital blow, the ground beneath my left foot seemed to collapse and my leg disappeared about seven inches from sight into a hole. Before I could move a muscle to free myself, out of the hole came a huge swarm of wasps, buzzing furiously and darting about at fever pitch to show their surprise and distaste for such a rude awakening. I do admit that I started the whole thing but, believe me, the last word certainly went to the wasps! Within a few seconds I'd been stung all over or, to be precise, in eleven different places. Thus, my felling test was brought to a rather sad end. Back at the camp, the first-aid kit was taken from its hidey-hole in the special tent known as The Office and my stings received medical attention.

One of my closest pals in the scout troup was Mickey Brennan, a lad with whom I had a lot in common. We both loved music and singing and, right from the start, got together for duets which we performed with great pleasure at campfires and scout concerts. I used to play the mandolin as our accompaniment until – I got my hands on a guitar.

This great ambition of mine became a reality when a neighbour of ours came back from working in a touring show, proudly carrying a lovely old instrument – the first guitar I'd ever seen in my life, apart from those in the films. This new acquisition, which I had on loan, opened up all sorts of joys to Mickey and I until, pretty soon, we were talked about round town.

You can imagine how thrilled we were one day when somebody contacted us to say that a concert was being organised at the Fisherman's Hall, in Dunmore East (the little village where I watched the regatta, if you remember), and that they would like Mickey and I to appear in it. The prospect of working on a stage, with the public sitting there watching us, made us feel like hardened pro's. So, right away, we set about preparing our contribution. The Fisherman's Hall was the first of many venues we were to play over the coming years.

Each summer there was a two-week fete in Waterford where, apart from all the usual fairground-type attractions, there were lots of dances, concerts and other live entertainments.

It was at these affairs that Mickey and I seemed to come into our own, finding ourselves being called upon for all kinds of public appearances.

A milestone in my life was reached when the names 'Doonican & Brennan' were suggested for a show in the adjoining town of New Ross. The difference was, on this occasion, that we would be paid for our trouble. Without the slightest worry about losing our 'amateur status', we travelled there with the others in the cast – all of us crammed into the back of a small van, bubbling with excitement. We did the concert and got ten shillings – between the two of us. My first salary as an entertainer!

5 'If I had a Hammer'

I was very unhappy about my mother having to work so hard and I gradually became more and more determined, come what may, to end my schooling and find some sort of job. Jobs were few and far between and, needless to say, the first area of investigation was the place where my father and two brothers, Ned and John, had worked. Ned made some enquiries initially and nothing was forthcoming but he was told that if anything did come along they'd let him know.

The company was called 'Graves' but didn't, as its name might suggest, specialize in making tombstones or running a burial service. It was, in fact, a pretty all round set-up, with several departments. The works was fronted by showrooms displaying and selling such items as bathroom fittings, tiled fireplaces, decorators' supplies, gardening tools and so on. Next you found the sawmill, with its high-pitched wailing sounds and that lovely smell of fresh sawdust. I loved going in there, passing along the alleyways between rows of neatly piled timbers lying to dry and season in preparation for their eventual sale. The sawyers, who worked in the mill, were a rather glamorous group of people to an impressionable young lad such as I was; the ones with the odd finger or two missing being the real heroes!

The next building was the ironmongery store, whose alleyways ran between rack upon rack of such things as nuts, bolts, nails, screws, hooks, hinges, door-knobs and hundreds of other delights. I didn't particularly like it, however; it was cold and uninviting compared with the sawmills and had a horrible oily smell. Round the corner was the 'box shop' – a department where machines, manned mainly by young lads, would assemble boxes and crates of all shapes and sizes. There, the finished products would sit in neatly arranged piles waiting to be delivered to local fish merchants, nurserymen, margarine manufacturers, or poultry farmers, whose names would be stamped in gay colours on the sides of their orders.

Next door was the steelworks (where my dad had spent his working-life and my brother Ned was now a foreman), this, in turn, was broken up into several sections, each specializing in different techniques including structural work, agricultural machines, such as farm trailers, wrought-iron gates and so on.

The whole place backed on to the river and had an extensive wharf where deliveries of wood or steel were made – its huge crane hovering above it like some hungry dinosaur having its dinner. Also suspended over the river was a long row of gents toilets – nothing more than a wooden shed containing a long seat with six or seven holes in it. This area was known appropriately enough among the lads as the 'Rear', a title, I hasten to add, inspired not by its use but by its location.

I was overjoyed when Ned came home one day with the news that there was a vacancy for a young lad in the 'box shop', and that I was to go and have an interview with one of the bosses some few days later. I was there on time but was not, as I expected, ushered into an office and told to sit down. Instead, I waited in the hallway until a door opened and the man whom I knew to be the boss walked out.

'Follow me,' he said, and moved briskly up the yard towards the box-making department.

I trailed along behind, feeling somewhat cheated that I didn't have to answer any questions, such as 'what's the square root of 121' – or 'what's the capital of Norway'.

The foreman of the boxshop met us as we entered. 'Good morning, sir,' he said to the boss, as he rubbed his hands together against the cold.

The boss said something quietly in reply then, waving a hand towards me, said 'Give this man a hammer, Jack,' and – with that – he left!

'Give this man a hammer'
The box factory where I got my first job, 1945-6

Jack was a nice man to have as a boss on your first job, for he was kind, understanding and good-humoured. He gave me a hammer; an instrument with which I became remarkably adept and I was soon knocking inch nails into boxes with such speed and accuracy that I would have made a worthy interlude on the 'Generation Game'.

I was soon able to use the box-making machines, and assist in other jobs, like stencilling the names on the various orders and loading them on to the lorries for delivery. My hours of work were from eight in the morning till five-thirty in the afternoon, except for Saturday, when we finished at twelve-thirty; my wages were twenty-two shillings and sixpence a week. (In today's currency, one pound, twelve and a halfpence!)

My brother Ned who, as I've told you, worked next door to where I was now employed, was very much aware of the lack of any kind of future for me in this firm, and constantly reminded me that I should think of it as temporary and strive for something better. But, how, what and where was anybody's guess.

After about a year of my new career knocking nails into boxes, I was told that there might be a vacancy for me in Ned's department; a move that was to bring me an extra pound per week. The prospect turned in to reality some weeks later and I started to learn something about putting iron girders together instead of pieces of timber. My early visits to the workshop with my father had already given me a useful familiarity with the place and its capabilities, so I rapidly got the hang of the simpler jobs. Naturally, Ned was a helpful boss but, as before, he never showed a great deal of enthusiasm for my presence there and was impatient for me to move on to something better!

One of the things I'll always remember about my first job, is something rather strange. All through my father's years of employment there, he would be presented each Christmas with an unusual bonus – the special gift to each of the senior members of the staff came in the form of 'Half a Pig's Head wrapped in Muslin'. My father would arrive home with this peculiar Christmas box tucked underneath his arm, its snout protruding forward giving the impression that the rest of the animal was behind struggling to free itself.

My mother would prepare and cook the thing for Christmas and I must say, with potatoes and cabbage, it was delicious – if a trifle fatty. I can tell you, from personal experience, that the old adage 'Making a silk purse out of a sow's ear' has a special meaning for me. I've sat chewing a piece of pig's ear, as other kids would their bubble-gum, and the best description I can give you is 'a gristle sandwich'. Mind you, I've never tried to chew a silk purse – so maybe my argument is not quite valid after all.

It was around that time (while I was at Graves) that I met Bruce Clarke. He played piano locally and was also very keen on the guitar. Somebody told him of my love of music, and the guitar in particular, so, happily, he sought me out. He came from England; his parents' home was in

70

Mansfield, near Nottingham, I think. Bruce's father came to Waterford and was, at that time, managing the biggest iron foundry in the area. Bruce was a 'pattern maker' by trade and was very clever indeed at making things. During the time I worked with him, he built his own guitars and also constructed a caravan in which we eventually travelled with a touring show.

The Clarke family lived in a fine house in Tramore situated on the cliff tops, looking out to sea and it was there that I began to spend a lot of my time when Bruce and I became friends. A couple of evenings a week, guitar in hand, I would board the Tramore Train and make that familiar journey to the seaside, the only difference being that now, for the first time in my life, I was learning what it felt like to travel there at night. Most of the time I would have the train practically to myself and, sitting there in the dimly lit carriage, I often took the opportunity of having my final moments of practice. On arrival, I would walk the three-quarters of a mile or so up the hill to Bruce's home where we'd begin our evening's get-together.

Half-way through our practice his mother would often call us to the kitchen, where she would treat us to tea and delicious cake made from broken biscuits and chocolate. When she discovered how I loved her speciality, she often handed me a special portion, wrapped in paper, to take home.

Our sessions together took us through a whole world of contrasting music with Bruce playing piano and steel guitar. His versatility combined with my singing and playing, allowed us to enter the different worlds of country and western material, pop songs of the time, folk music, Hawaiian numbers and, of course, jazz. Pretty soon our repertoire became quite impressive and the months of devoted practice rapidly extended my musical knowledge and ability.

Of course my partner worked at his 'proper' job during the day, earning his living as a pattern-maker, but he never tried to conceal the fact that his heart wasn't in it. It was more than obvious to me and everybody else that music was the most important thing in his life. Each week we'd await the arrival in the post of our copy of *The Melody Maker* – keeping up to date on who was doing what, with which band and where. The local music store became a regular haunt and helped to keep us supplied with our needs in guitar and piano music, not to mention gramophone records. It was on one of our many visits there, that the lady in charge informed us of a very exciting event which was on the musical horizon.

It appeared that, some three weeks hence, a man would be coming down from Dublin with a mobile recording unit and would be happy to record any local talent that had the courage and financial wherewithal to have a go. We put our names on the list immediately and were assured that, as soon as the appointments were being dished out, the lady would let us know. As far as I remember, we were allowed to record a double-sided record for 'thirty bob' – or one pound, fifty pence.

With great excitement and determination we made our plans, deciding to launch ourselves into the recording world as instrumentalists. 'Out of Nowhere', a popular song of the period, was our choice for one side – with Bruce playing piano to my guitar – and we decided to join forces on guitar (Bruce playing steel) in a Hawaiian Medley on the flip side.

After a few weeks of regular rehearsals, we received the anxiously awaited appointment card from the music shop telling us to be there at 10.30 am the following Wednesday. Well, glad to say, our efforts were highly praised by the recording engineer; a man we were to meet up with again in later years. Proudly we wrapped up the precious evidence of our many weeks of hard work. Thank goodness Bruce had the money to pay for it – because I didn't!

Over the following months we played the thing a thousand times and, even though we were warned that the heavy-gauge needle in our old-fashioned radiograms would wear the disc out rather quickly, I'm glad to say that last time I saw Bruce at his present home in Norfolk he still had it.

One of the other budding stars to invest thirty shillings in his career on that occasion, was my old pal Mickey Brennan. He tells me that he has tried, time and time again, to retrieve the record from his mother and destroy the evidence but 'she's so proud of her lad' that the poor fellow's got no chance.

With this experience behind us, we decided to try our luck at entering the world of broadcasting. Each week we listened, with great interest to the regular talent show 'Beginners Please' which was broadcast on Radio Eireann, our national station. We wondered what our chances would be and, after some initial discussion, Bruce sent a letter to the programme planners putting our names forward as prospective candidates for the show.

In due course we did an audition and were accepted, so, once again, we went into training. Two contrasting items were chosen for our spot: a steel guitar solo featuring Bruce and a song from me to follow. It went very well indeed and, for many years afterwards, I treasured a recording of the occasion: my first broadcast and a milestone in my life.

Slowly I began to collect the odd gramophone record that appealed to me and, where once the household was lulled to the romantic strains of 'Whispering', sung by The Comedy Harmonists, the mood now changed to the more up-tempo ryhthms of 'The Quintet Of The Hot Club Of France' featuring Django Reinhardt on guitar and Stephane Grappelli on violin. Stephane is now a professional friend and colleague having worked several times as a guest on my television shows but as far as I know he's completely unaware of the nostalgia his presence creates. After all, in his particular case I'm one of many millions of admirers who've loved him since childhood, so I've never bothered to stress the point.

Many, many, times I've expressed how strongly I feel

about the whole idea of meeting and working with people you've loved and admired, from afar, through your lifetime; it's very important to me. When I started out on my efforts to sing songs to guitar accompaniment, I took every possible opportunity to listen to all the people who were, at that time, setting the standards.

One such name was the legendary Burl Ives. I collected his records and books of songs, using his material as the foundation stone of my early repertoire. Pretty soon I was entertaining my family with my own rendition of such songs as 'The Blue-Tailed Fly' and 'Mr Frog Went A Courtin'', always trying to copy the guitar sounds supplied by the expert session-guitarists assisting the 'master' on his recordings.

Some years later, when I was playing in a band in Dublin, I was informed one evening, by the manager of the hotel where we worked, that the great man would be appearing there later in the year. When the time finally came round we discovered he didn't want the band on stage so, greatly disappointed, I had to content myself with a glimpse of the back of his head - as I looked through the door of the bandroom - and nothing more. However, in 1971, he flew over from the States to appear on my show and, this time, things were very different.

One evening we sat in the sitting-room of my home, together with our wives, and talked at great length of our mutual love of our work.

'You tell me you've got children,' he said.

'Yes, two daughters,' I told him.

'I'd just love to see them,' he went on. 'Are they in bed?'

'Yes, they are,' my wife Lynn said, 'but you're more than welcome to see them, if you'd like to. They won't be asleep yet.'

'I'd sure like that,' he responded, rising from his chair by the fire.

We headed upstairs to the children's bedroom where the girls sat up in surprise to stare at their huge bearded visitor.

They were aged about five and four at the time and said little, just sucked their thumbs through nervous smiles. Burl sat on the bed and chatted to them then, without the slightest encouragement, gently began to sing, 'Fuzzy Wuzzy was a bear – Fuzzy Wuzzy had no hair'. The girls continued to stare in wonderment.

As for me, I stood at the foot of the bed thinking to myself: 'How about that, Burl Ives sitting on the edge of my children's bed singing just for them.' The sad part was that they hadn't the faintest idea who he was!

I've often described the incident as 'The greatest waste of excitement I've ever known'. I felt I should climb into the bed myself, simply to satisfy my memory.

Burl returned to appear on my show in 1979 and, this time, my daughters were able to appreciate the whole thing much more as we sat in his dressing-room at the studios.

My relationship with Bruce Clarke led, quite naturally somehow, to my first professional engagement. It was in the summer of 1947, a job playing and singing in a quartet, led by Bruce himself. The venue was a ballroom at a tiny seaside resort called Courtown Harbour, on the south-east coast of Ireland.

Now that I'd secured my first contract in the world of music, I had some very important details to attend to. You see, I still didn't possess a guitar of my own and a fully-fledged professional guitarist-vocalist, with no guitar, was, to say the least, unsatisfactory. Up to that time a friend of mine, whose parents had a guitar in the attic, with no intention of ever dusting same, kindly allowed me to have the loan of it.

Bruce and I saw in the music papers that a man in Dublin, whom we knew to be a guitar teacher and one of the few guitarists of any note in Ireland, had a good quality Gibson guitar for sale. The price was twenty pounds – a sum of money that, to me, at that time, would have built Concorde; I didn't have twenty pence to my name. But the season in prospect was security enough for Bruce to offer to lend me the money. I agreed to pay it back, at the rate of two pounds a week, while we worked together for the summer. So my first problem was solved. I wrote to the man in Dublin, sent a deposit and offered to come up and collect my prize the following week. He agreed and I started to prepare for the trip.

I was nineteen years old then and, incredibly, had never been on such a long journey – one hundred miles from my home. I got the twenty pounds together, then started to work out how much more cash I would need for the return train journey – this was problem number two. I managed to scrape together half the required sum, knowing that I only had a week to make good the rest. One of my family gave me the tip that a shopkeeper in town drove to Dublin on a certain day each week and that he might possibly be able to come to my rescue.

I appeared in his shop the next morning and asked if I could speak to him. He was very charming and said he'd love to oblige but he'd already promised a lift to somebody else and, besides, would have to stay overnight in Dublin, which would be too expensive for me. I immediately assured him that I would gladly come back on the train, in the early evening, knowing that I had the single fare. He must have been touched by the urgency in my argument, because he scratched his head and said, 'Ah! well, I suppose you could go in the back of the van with the load. Mind you, there are no windows and it's very bumpy – it's up to you.' Without hesitation, I asked what time he would be leaving and then, having arranged to be outside the shop at 8.30 am, I rushed home with my heart pounding.

I could never have anticipated the discomfort I suffered on that journey – the twisting and turning on the country roads, as I sat huddled between some wooden crates, was horrific. I was sick twice, and had no way of letting the driver in the front know of my predicament!

Anyway, as I've told you, I was a great radio fan in those days and one of my heroes was Ireland's leading guitarist, Jack Gregory. Knowing that I would be in Dublin for a whole day I had taken the opportunity of writing to him

76

also, asking if I could possibly meet him. I explained that I was trying to learn, on my own, from books, and that a few words of encouragement would go a long way. I had a letter from Jack, telling me to meet him at his place of work at 4 pm. (At the time he was featured guitarist with the resident orchestra at one of Dublin's top ballrooms, The Four Provinces.) The day had so much in store for this young man from the country that the misery he suffered in the van was only part payment for the subsequent rewards.

It seemed like a lifetime before the dreadful rumbling stopped, the van squeaked to a standstill and the back door opened to let in my first glimpse of Dublin sunshine. The driver, now aware of my discomposure, sympathized and helped me to my feet. It took my legs quite a while to unfold into their normal position but I soon forgot it all as I walked along the street in search of a Bus Stop where I made some enquiries about getting to Rathmines district.

When I got there, I was received by the man selling the guitar. He invited me into his front room, offered me a cup of tea and then produced a magnificent, black, shiny guitar. It really was superb. I sat down and fondled it for a while, hardly believing it was to be mine. While the tea was on its way, I played through my limited repertoire of chords and licks stopping, from time to time, to hold my pride and joy up to the light and have another look. I said goodbye at the door and walked away, carrying my new partner lovingly in its black glossy case.

I was on top of the world. I walked for ages and remember well passing a park and being tempted to sit on the bench and have another play. I had some fish and chips instead, as I sat on the park bench, and watched the time as it approached my afternoon date with my guitar hero.

Dead on time, he was standing at the entrance to the ballroom when I got there. He took me inside, where the lights on the bandstand had been especially turned on. What a very fancy place, I thought, as Jack went to his dressing-room and returned carrying a magnificent electric guitar. He plugged it in and just handed it to me. 'Let's see what you can do then,' he said smiling. 'Go on, don't be nervous,' I was – very nervous!

Sitting down, I started to finger the guitar and, as I did so, he opened up the guitar book on the music stand (that's the folder containing all the guitar parts for the band's library of music), picked a part at random and said, 'Try that,' Feeling very inadequate, I slowly played my way through it and when I finally looked up for some sort of approval, he simply turned the music over and said, 'Great, try this one.' He then asked me to get my new guitar which, by the way, he knew. 'It is a good one,' he said, 'and I know most of the good ones in town.'

We played together for about an hour. I don't think I can recall any other hour in my musical life which gave me such confidence and inspiration. When he saw me off at the end of our interlude, I was not to know that – in a very few years – Jack and I would be doing duets on the radio. I heard from him quite recently and he's still helping young people with their efforts to be better guitarists.

At seven o'clock that evening, I boarded the train back to Waterford and thought that I would never get home quickly enough to show my family my treasured instrument. I sat playing till the early hours of the next morning; that guitar and my hands, in fact, rarely parted company for the next five or six years. Well, I was set for my first job – I managed to borrow an amplifier, until such time as I could buy one of my own, so, for better or for worse, I was a Professional.

Five pounds a week was to be my reward according to Bruce, plus my food. With that money I was able to pay the instalments on my first guitar, send two pounds a week to my family and keep a pound for myself. I was in show business; I was loving it; and I was never to leave it.

I practised for about six hours every day while I was doing this first season and made up my mind to learn as much as I could, every day, about this great new world of which I'd become a part. When the season was nearing its close, I started to get the feeling that my career was running-out too, since there was no sign of any other job on the horizon.

Then out of the blue, came an engagement which numbers amongst the most peculiar I have ever undertaken. In Ireland, in the mid-to-late forties, the tax on cinema seats was raised to a level that made all the movie house owners look around for a way of avoiding the evils of the tax laws. One of the escapes came in a form known as cine-variety; what this really meant was that if the film on show at the time was accompanied by live entertainment, the taxes didn't come into operation.

What a blessing this turned out to be for Bruce and myself. Working in our little summer venue of Courtown Harbour we were approached by a ballroom and cinema proprietor from a neighbouring town. He wanted to use our talent to help avoid his cinema tax; in other words, we were to be the variety side of things. We asked him about the length of time we were required to be on stage and were absolutely staggered to find that the law required our contribution to be at least as long as the film. Since the feature films were about an hour and forty-five minutes it presented us with the most impossible task.

It's one thing playing for people to dance but it's vastly different when your audience are sitting down just listening. Anyway, jobs were not things to be turned down because you couldn't do them, the answer was to say, 'Yes please,' and then spend the remainder of the engagement getting yourself out of trouble.

Bruce and I sat down and worked out endless programmes of songs, instrumental duets, etc., that would fill in part of the time at least. This, by the way, was before we'd done variety shows or radio series so we weren't going into the thing with a ready-made library or any such luxury. But, more power to our elbows, we tackled the thing bravely, only to find that the situation had many hidden problems which we were yet to discover.

The film began showing in the early afternoon and

played three times, which meant that we had to do about six hours of stage work each day – as the variety side came before the film, we would be on the stage at about one-thirty in the afternoon. Now in a country town the chances of having an audience, at that time, were non-existent but what we didn't reckon on was that we did the the odd member of the unemployed who, I presume, the boss allowed in for nothing, if only to show them that there were worse things than being out of work.

Some days there were as many as four people in the auditorium: two drunks and a lady doing her knitting, while her little grand-daughter tucked her dolly up in a blanket on one of the empty seats.

After a few days the afternoon audience 'dropped off', until nobody came in at all, so Bruce and I would sit on stage and talk. I would then go off for a while and Bruce would practice his scales. After that, we'd reverse the routine, each of us in turn keeping an eye on the door, if an audience came in we'd get together and try to entertain him, or her. The five o'clock show would be a bit more natural and once our final stint was over, we'd sit and watch the film.

I'll always remember our digs in that town. The landlady was an elderly woman who kept her money in her stockings – while she was wearing them. I don't mean she slipped a few neatly folded pound notes into her stocking tops à la Sophia Loren, she simply scrunched them up and pushed them down anywhere she found a space. The overall effect was a pair of legs that looked like a very good crop of brussels sprouts.

She served our meals in the front-room which had that familiar mouldy smell of damp. On the wall was a picture of an old gentleman, some relation or other, in a large frame; he had a bowler hat, a moustache and a fly-away collar. Like so many of those old faded sepia photos, he wore a look of total astonishment on his face, as though somebody had just kicked his shins as the picture was taken. Day by day we grew to resent that stare in his eyes, which watched our every move and gave the impression that he was hearing our every word.

The landlady must have had an admirer in the sausage trade (he was probably kinky about legs full of money) because we seemed to get them very often. We began to leave quite a few on our plates, so she nagged us about it, 'All the trouble I go to, cooking good food for you lads...' etc. Come to think of it, we were ungrateful pups because she fed us well and charged us very little. I suppose I can put it down to youth, or something.

One day, Bruce picked up a left-over sausage and threw it at the picture scoring a direct hit on his bowler. My shot was not so good and would have disappeared over his shoulder. In fact, that's precisely where the 'banger' finished because we just dropped the occasional one down behind the picture. I don't know if she ever decorated the room but, if she did, I'm sure her relative was glad to get the weight off his shoulders.

At the end of this unique engagement, with no work in the book, Bruce and I had little to do but get back to our musical get-togethers in Tramore, while during the daytime he was busy putting the finishing touches to the caravan he'd been building in his front garden.

His job completed, he hitched it up to his old Morris car and took it for its first road test. It was perfect. As we sped along by the deserted promenade, Bruce broke the news that he'd been offered a job with a small touring show, one of those known in the trade as a 'fit-up'. Travelling from one small town, or village, to another, these small companies played the local church hall, cinema, or anywhere else suitable for a performance. More often than not a makeshift stage would have to be erected especially for the occasion, hence the name 'fit-up'.

The company usually consisted of about five or six people, who between them supplied all the required talents for the proposed entertainment.

You might have the boss of the outfit as the comedian, his wife who sang, danced, acted, or played the piano, a son or daughter who did likewise, an accordian player who also did a magical act, and his wife who sang and took part in sketches. Their combined talents gave you, the orchestra, a variety bill for the first half, and the cast of a one-act play for the second part of the evening's presentation.

Bruce was engaged to tour with them for a season of several weeks, playing accordian, piano (if there was one) and any other duties the boss might suggest.

Since the deal did not include me, it meant the end of our musical association, at least for a while. But, a week or so before the opening date, Bruce hinted that since I had nothing better to do, I might like to go along for the ride. I agreed, on condition that I would pay my way as far as possible, sharing food bills and so on. The following week we were on the road heading towards the border with Northern Ireland. The tour was to be just south of the border.

While Bruce did his show at the village hall I'd stay behind, cooking some sort of evening meal on the simple coal stove, the windows steaming up and a plume of back smoke coming from our little chimney. Some kind lady would do our laundry for us, hanging it out on the bushes to dry in the sun while we, at every opportunity, would pop down to the hall and practise our music.

Come to think of it, if we did the same thing today eyebrows would be raised. The very idea of two fellows travelling about in a caravan with only one of them working. We'd soon be known as the 'odd couple'. We never gave it a second thought. Times have changed.

Some evenings I'd wander down, stand at the back of the hall and watch as the boss nipped around between stage appearances to count the takings; the audience having a great time. Many of the halls were so tiny you wondered how they could possibly make any money.

I did learn one thing though, and that is: don't judge the intelligence of your audience by the size of the hall. As my dear friend Arthur Askey would say, 'Just because there's not many in, you don't have to work half-hearted.'

6 'Where the hell's E Flat?'

Fortunately, the summer of '48 presented no problem as we were both invited to return to Courtown Harbour for another season. Then Bruce came across an advertisement, in a music paper, offering employment to a 'pianist' and a 'drummer' in one of the more successful provincial bands in Ireland. I had never played drums in my life, except for some light-hearted fun playing a kettle drum in the Scouts' band, but my keenness to stay in the music world, and also to continue my association with Bruce, led to my next undertaking.

I applied for the job as drummer with the band (who, luckily had their own drum kit), got a favourable reply and then spent the last few weeks of my summer season practising night, noon and morning, in order to equip myself for the awesome task ahead. My knowledge of music made it easy for me to follow the drum parts used in orchestras and bands, but my complete lack of technique made the effort of playing, for any longer than twenty minutes or so, quite exhausting.

However, I joined the band and, good or bad, I stayed with them for six months playing one-night stands seven nights a week, practically without a break. Some quite incredible things were in store for me as a drummer and all very good experience for a young apprentice. The first 'gig' I did with them was a six-hour dance in a place called Dungarven, some twenty-five or thirty miles from my home. For a start, it took me a painful length of time to assemble the drum kit which they supplied, since it was something I hadn't done before and for which, sadly, I was not prepared. That evening was a nightmare, to say the least.

After one hour of my tense fumbling efforts, I felt completely demoralised and ashamed, convinced that when the dance ended I'd be sent on my way with an evening's payment and a curt goodbye! By some happy twist of fate the bandleader was unable to be there that evening and left things in the hands of his assistant, Davey, who drove the limousine, chose the evening's programme and was also one of the band's vocalists. Maybe it was because he had so much on his mind that his judgement was dulled, but he certainly treated me well and gave me some badly needed moral support.

The dance began at nine o'clock and by about eleven-thirty my right foot, which was working the bass drum pedal, had become totally paralysed. Try as I may, I could get nothing more than a few nervous twitches from the ankle joint so decided to leave the ground floor portion of my drumming to rest in peace, and manage with my poor aching upper-half. When the evening was finally over and all the gear packed in our trailer, we headed north towards the town where the band was based. After a few fitful hours of rest, I had to go and meet my new boss.

He welcomed me and hoped I wasn't too tired after my ordeal on the previous night and, over some tea, told me my pay would be two pounds a night and that we would be working almost every night of the week.

The travelling was to prove exhausting as indeed were those long six-hour dances but, in my youthful dedication, I still studied music and practised my guitar for hours every day.

The popularity of the band always impressed me and, through it, I learned one of my first vital lessons. When you entertain the public it's no good just having good music or singing, you must also have entertainment value, so people will go home having had a good time. The band itself left a lot to be desired musically, as you'll gather from the quality of my contribution at the time but, over all, it gave great value to the patrons and showed me that my boss had his finger on the commercial pulse.

He knew that I was working hard at music –

particularly the guitar – and often tried to persuade me to think more commercially, reminding me that, in those days, the guitar was a bad choice of instrument. (Admittedly, even in the semi-professional world, there were just a handful of people in Ireland who tried to play the guitar.)

Every now and then he would allow me to play a guitar solo with the band but it invariably had the 'novelty' approach associated with more unorthodox instruments such as the zither or the balalaika. Looking back on those days now, it's hard to believe the rarity of the guitar considering the enormity of its popularity today. As the weeks went by I worked hard to improve my efforts on the drums and, though I never achieved any degree of skill, my playing became workmanlike and I didn't feel I was getting money under false pretences. The sadness was, that I never really wanted to be a drummer, so I didn't get any pleasure from playing.

The man I was working for at the time was a remarkable character; a heavily built man who played piano and who, when in action, always looked to me like a white Fats Waller. He hosted the band with great skill and certainly knew all the tricks of the trade when it came to pleasing the public.

I don't know whether it was because he was getting older or not, but his moods seemed to change dramatically and his behaviour at times was, to a young, inexperienced, newcomer like myself, quite alarming.

One of the first things he told me on joining the band was that there were three rules he liked adhered to at all times.

Rule 1. You must not drink any alcohol during working hours.

Rule 2. You must not associate with members of the opposite sex, during working hours.

Rule 3. (And how about this!) You must not talk about music while travelling to and from various jobs.

Needless to say, the third rule was by far the most difficult one to obey, since conversations about music is on the lips of musicians at all times.

During the period I spent with the band, I learned more about the geography of Ireland than I ever did at school. Travelling the length and breadth of the country, week in week out, I began to build-up a picture in my mind of the twenty-six counties of Southern Ireland and the six of Northern Ireland – much more enlightening than that coloured jigsaw we were so familiar with in the classroom. The small towns and villages – up till then, nothing more than names from my exercise book – came to life as we drove through them and have remained in my memory ever since.

One summer's evening we arrived in Longford to play at the C.I.E. Annual Dance. The initials, C.I.E., are an abbreviation of the name 'Corus Iompar Eireann' which is the Gaelic name for, what is best described as the Irish equivalent of British Transport. But, just a moment. I've realised that I can't tell you the following story without, first including a supplementary anecdote vital to its maximum effect.

I have told you earlier about the bandleader's assistant who looked after the band, drove the limousine, took responsibility for the music and also sang some of the vocals in a typical Irish tenor voice. Well, the boss got the bright idea there was yet another chore Davey could handle for the betterment of our set-up.

We didn't have a string bass in the band and, since many of the touring groups were sporting this vital instrument, the boss decided – in spite of its size and awkwardness in transport – that he'd have one.

I don't know if this came about because he happened across one which was going cheap, or because he really felt it would give our outfit an extra touch of class. Either way, in no time, there it was.

The boss insisted that it came with us on the day it was acquired and promptly instructed Davey to play it in between songs.

'I don't know one note from another,' he said indignantly.

'Who's gonna know whether you do or not?' said the boss. 'You can't really hear them, anyway.'

So Davey became a bass player.

Whenever he suspected that there were any musicians in the hall, he'd make that extra effort and shout to me, 'What key are we in?'

I'd look puzzled and say, 'How the hell do I know, I'm playing the drums.'

To put him out of his misery, I'd look over the boss's shoulder and examine the piano copy, 'E flat,' I'd shout to Davey.

'Where's E flat on the bass?' he'd ask, with a twinkle in his eye.

'Oh! about eight inches up on that second string,' I'd say and then I'd watch Davey grab the appropriate spot and knock hell out of it right through the number. Of course, Davey never even tuned the strings up so he couldn't possibly play a right note anyway – even by accident. For months after that, however, he played the bass every night!

And that enables me to take you back to the C.I.E. dance at Longford. We arrived good and early and set up at the hall which was gaily decorated with bunting, fancy banners and lanters. Added to those was a long criss-cross of ribbon which zig-zagged right down the entire length of the hall, carrying – at intervals of about two feet – a series of cards bearing numbers from one to one hundred. These were to be used as a means of choosing winners of spot-prizes (every now and then the band-leader would stop the music and say, 'The couple standing under card number eighty-five,' which usually invited a mad scramble to the bandstand, where the lucky couple would get a packet of cigarettes and a pair of nylon stockings). I had completed the assembling of the drums while all the other fellows were placing chairs, music-stands, microphones, instruments and so on, in their correct positions, ready for action.

It had been arranged, when we'd got everything ready, that we would go to some local lodgings or hotel where we would have something to eat before the six-hour slog began.

A group of the organising committee stationed themselves at a vantage point, quite near the bandstand, in order to watch the famous visiting orchestra go through their daily routine and they seemed most impressed by what they saw. The boss, who was sitting by the bandstand, began to talk to them asking various questions about how many people were coming etc., then, quite without warning, he turned to the bandstand and said, 'Gentlemen, can I have your attention for a minute?'

We felt sure he was going to say, 'Will bacon and egg be OK for the lot of ya?' But no – something followed which was such a bolt from the blue, that it left all of us quite speechless.

He stood there, his hands in his overcoat pockets, then, like an army officer addressing his troops, began to pace up and down, 'Lads,' he said, 'I feel I must bring this up – much as I hate to do it – I've got to get it off my mind.' Then a pause ... 'The intonation of the band has been very, very, bad lately. I've been ashamed, at times, that so little care has been taken in tuning-up. So, as from now, it's got to be put right.'

With these words he climbed on to the bandstand, sat at the piano, gave one of the notes a most fearful thump and said, 'Now, everybody, tune-up!' There must have been ten seconds of shocked silence before a rather awkward fumbling for saxes, trumpets and trombones broke the deathly hush and then followed some weird 'tweeting' of notes. The boss was in full cry now – he kept bashing the poor note on the piano, making it more difficult for the lads by playing the wrong note for normal tuning-up.

'Come on, Bob,' he'd shout to the trumpet. 'You too, Sean – come on Liam.'

All the boys were madly tuning-up, to his thunderous piano note, as Davey climbed on to the stand carrying a pile of music.

My sole picture of Dad. He looks about 20 here which would make the date 1898.

My mother, as I remember her during my school years.

The Doonicans outside the Hut in 1933. Back row: (left to right) Ned, John; middle row: Nancy, Mom, Nellie, Lar; front row: me, Una, Mary.

A camping holiday with two of my pals, Derry and John, on Lord Waterford's estate in Stradbally. This was the first guitar I ever played, borrowed from a neighbour.

At the Dublin spring show in 1950. One of the show's main attractions was a demonstration of closed-circuit television given by Pye; this was probably the first time television of any sort had appeared in Ireland. Bruce (on piano), my first professional partner, and I were one of the televised acts. *(Studio 1, Dublin)*

The caravan that Bruce built for our first ever tour in 1946-7.
As the cook, I slaved over a tiny coal stove inside the caravan which then became like an oven itself.

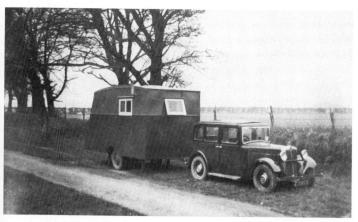

Above: The Four Ramblers—1955 vintage. (Left to right): Peter Roy, Frank Davies (of the squeaky boots) and my friend Dee. The good-looking chap at the back is me.

An artist's impression in one of the Dublin evening papers of the Bobby Murphy band about 1950. This was one of the last bands I played with before I left Ireland.

Above: Lynn rehearsing pantomime in Birmingham with Eric and Ernie, and the famous pantomime dame, George Lacy. I spent most of that season as a stage-door Johnny waiting to date the principal boy. *(Birmingham Post & Mail)*

Lynn with Harry Secombe when she appeared in his 'Large as Life' show which had a very successful run at the London Palladium in the late '50s. *(Newcastle Chronicle & Journal Ltd)*

The new Doonican
family, 1968.
Fiona and Sarah
(with Lynn) wave to
their fans.
*(Graham Hooper,
Torquay)*

Finding myself a
seat. *(Ron Howard)*

The kind of company I never dreamed I'd keep. Doing the 1969
summer season at the Opera House, Blackpool with (left to right)
Arthur Worsley, John Hanson, Sid James, Mrs Mills, Cilla Black,
Arthur Askey, Moira Anderson, Charlie Cairoli, Violet Carson,
Jimmy Clitheroe and Roy Castle. *(H. A. Hallas, Blackpool)*

Teeing off with my friend Eric Sykes against American actors,
George C. Scott and Steve Forrest. (We won.) Gleneagles, 1976.
(Ian Joy, St. Andrews)

One of my favourite shots, but they weren't coming to see my show. The Royal Performance took place during my season at the London Palladium in 1970. *(Joe Matthews)*

A memorable and very moving occasion during a holiday in Rome in the early '70s. *(Pontificia Fotografia)*

'Davey, will you put that music down and tune-up,' he bellowed.

Davey looked up from his crouching position, 'What's that?' he said.

'Get your bass and tune-up,' the boss insisted.

Poor Davey, he'd never even taken up the slack on those strings since he got it. 'Are you coddin' me?' he asked, half laughing but, immediately, knew he'd said the wrong thing with the committee members almost within earshot.

He put the music on to the floor and, with a look of complete terror in his eyes, picked up the bass. Now, to start with, the machines for tightening the strings were rusty, the strings themselves were ancient and, worst of all, Davey wouldn't know the right note even if he heard it. However, he was out of his depth now and had to sink or swim.

He grabbed the most convenient machine-head and started to turn it; as he laboured over his operation with his left hand, his right hand gently plucked the string which was giving out a sort of low belching sound. The rest of the band sat down, fascinated by the operation and wondering what the outcome would eventually be. After a whole minute of turning the creaking machine-head, the string had tightened up sufficiently to produce a recognisable note. But, the relationship between the note the boss was playing, the note the bass was producing and the note that Davey would eventually settle for, was something that filled us all with expectation.

Davey lost his nerve after a bit and discreetly switched to one of the other machines, which was so stiff that he decided to settle for the devil he knew. The string had now tuned-up so high that you could almost see it getting thinner, and it was beginning to sound like a guitar string. Little friendly whispers began to advise the tuner, 'Don't go any higher, Davey.' 'Tell him you can't turn it any more.' 'The string is going to break.' The boss was beginning to look as though he knew he'd done the wrong thing but was in too deep. All he could do, in front of the committee, was keep on until something happened. And something certainly did happen.

There was an almighty bang as the tailpiece of the bass could no longer take the strain; the piece of wire which attached the tailpiece to the knob underneath snapped. The action that then took place was similar to that of a catapult: the whole tail section flew into the air like a slingshot, hitting the decorations over the bandstand, snapping the ribbons. The result, was incredible. Just like a line of falling dominoes, the zigzag bunting and numbered cards began to fall, first at the top of the hall, where we all sat aghast, then – by degrees – right down to the other end. I shall never forget the sight of the committee members as they stood there, motionless, with the multi-coloured decorations strewn over their heads and shoulders. That, as far as I remember, was the end of Davey's career as a bass player. Well, a fully-tuned-up-one anyway.

In some of the more remote areas of Ireland, dances, of any importance, were looked upon as quite an occasion for the entire population. It was fascinating to arrive and find all the seats around the hall taken by children and the very old members of the community. Grannies in their Sunday best, with their pipe-smoking companions, sat there just listening to the band tuning-up and looking forward to a kind of orchestral concert. They'd watch the younger people dance and enjoy themselves until such time as they – and the children – felt it was time for bed. Then home they'd go.

The introduction of the Crystal Ball and its fairyland effects, made it all rather a dreamlike experience for the non-dancers. The Crystal Ball (many of which, I'm told, have been retrieved from junk-rooms and restored for use at discos), for the uninitiated, was about the size of a large football, its surface covered with tiny mirror-squares which reflected the glow from the spotlight trained on it. As the ballroom lights were lowered and the ball began to revolve, the effect was like hundreds of stars flickering round the room.

Another indelible memory of those nights, back in the forties, was the 'smell' of the dance halls. Some of the places we played had not yet found the more sophisticated methods of giving the dance floor its shiny-slippery surface, so the traditional method was often used. This was the routine: before the patrons arrived for the evening's recreation, the caretaker would sprinkle a mixture of paraffin oil and candle-grease all around the floor then, by the time the first few dances were over, the whole thing was shining and gleaming like an ice-rink. I don't know where the oil and candles disappeared to as the evening passed, but I do know that the smell stayed with me for years. You could tell what job we were all in once you came within ten feet of our dinner jackets or overcoats. Many a funny look we got, as we walked into hotels or restaurants. People, who were not familiar with the ballroom smell, must have thought we were well-dressed mechanics or Parish Priests.

Anybody who has ever worked with me in the entertainment world – whether producer, director, script writer, musician or designer – will admit, I hope, that the one quality I do not lack is enthusiasm. I'm always keen to see that not only is my own contribution up to scratch but that any help I can give to anybody else is readily available. In these days of stringent trade-union ruling on any one man doing a job allocated to somebody else, this keenness of mine has had to be kept under control.

I've actually been told off for moving the rocking-chair I was sitting in to a more advantageous angle for the cameras. A voice from the side of the set quietly instructed me, 'You do the singin', mate, we'll move the props. OK?'

My keenness to do the right thing brought about one of my funniest experiences back in my ballroom days. We arrived one night at a very small country village in the west of Ireland. I started to cart the gear up through the

91

small village hall, with its familiar smell, and heard the usual echoing sounds of my heavy feet on the slippery floor. Small though the place was, it proudly possessed a shining Crystal Ball and I noticed, on this occasion, that immediately underneath it, in the centre of the floor, stood two large whitewood kitchen chairs!

I tried to guess what they were doing there but I was baffled; they were not tall enough for anybody to have placed them there in an effort to reach the Crystal Ball neither did they, in any way, match the other chairs around the walls.

When the dance finally got underway I watched with interest to see if, and when, they would be removed by one of the organisers of the function but nobody made any such move.

With each dance the floor got busier and, to all of us on the bandstand, the chairs appeared to be turning into quite a dangerous hazard. Couples in happy abandon went whizzing past them, missing them by inches, and by now the music and singing had become quite secondary as far as we were concerned. The chairs were the stars of the evening.

The first half ended and we made our way to the refreshment room where local ladies served us tea with homemade sandwiches and cakes.

I mentioned the, now infamous, chairs to the committee members, who just laughed, telling me not to worry about them. I even asked the boss if we should move them, but his reaction was, 'Oh! to hell with them, they've got nothing to do with us. If they want the things moved, let them do it themselves.'

The night was in full swing now and the boss decided it was time everybody really let loose in an Irish dance. A great favourite 'The Walls of Limerick' was announced and all the laughing couples rushed on to the floor, holding hands and shuffling into position. It was only then the boss felt some action should be taken – fearing that, in the frenzy of the next few minutes, the dancers would find it impossible to avoid the obstacle in the centre of the floor.

'I'll go down and move them to the side of the floor,' I offered, feeling that at last the nagging worry of the chairs would be gone. An announcement was made to the dancers to wait for just a minute. I stepped off the stand and started for the middle of the floor; the dancers moving aside to make way for me, at the same time giving a jeering round of applause. I took a chair in each hand and slid them at arms length to the side of the room, leaving them against the wall. Back on the stand, the time was being stomped-out by the boss's heavy foot and the 'Walls of Limerick' were scaled.

Suddenly, amid the happy laughing voices and the dancing feet, there was an almighty crashing sound, screaming voices brought the music to a stop and all eyes turned in the direction of the commotion. The committee members rushed to the middle of the hall, where the dancers stood surrounding a gaping hole in the centre of the floor.

It turned out that, a couple of nights before, some workmen had damaged a few of the floorboards and had not been able to fix them in time, so, what did they do? Like any decent workers they placed a warning sign and, as one of the patrons said, 'If that stupid 'eejit' in the band had left the chairs where they were – and minded his own business – nothing would have gone wrong!'

In these days of the disco craze, it's hard to imagine the ancient customs of the dance halls. The tango, the oldtime waltz and the Paul Jones – these rituals, strange as they may seem to the youngsters of today, were an absolute Must in the repertoire of any God-fearing Band who took to the road in those days. You ask a young drummer today to play a tango, rhumba, or even samba rhythm, and he's liable to think you're soft in the head.

One fateful tango (or should I say, set of tangos?) will remain in my memory for ever. I say 'set of tangos' since, as people who danced in the forties and fifties will know, the dance was announced – whether slow-waltz, foxtrot or quickstep – and you took your partner on the floor to dance to three successive tunes in that tempo.

We were playing at some ball or other one night and as the evening – and morning – wore on I played my way through dance after dance, feeling very sorry for myself as I had a stinking cold at the time. We had the order from the boss that the next dance would be a tango and we'd be playing Nos. 41, 56 and 60, from our library. We all rooted out the parts, put them on the stands and, without any warning, there came a loud, 'a-one-two-three-four', from the direction of the piano and off we went.

I had been taken by surprise and hadn't had the opportunity of blowing my nose, which was now dribbling and running completely out of control. I groped in my trouser pocket, lifting my bottom off the stool to do so and, at the same time, kept playing the tango with one hand. I managed to free the hankie from my creased-up pocket and desperately clapped it to my nose, before I dripped on to my drum skins. While I was enjoying a much needed blow, there came a ferocious shout from the other side of the stand, 'STOP!' The music came to a staggering halt and everybody looked towards the boss in amazement. The audience also looked up, smiling all over their faces and shuffling nearer to what they thought was a 'spot-prize position'.

They were only to be entertained by the following strange banter, between the boss and me:

Boss: (shouting) 'What's all this about?'
Me: (hoarse) 'What's all what about?'
Boss: 'Blowing your nose during a tango!'
Me: 'I didn't know there was any rule about blowing your nose during a tango.'
Boss: 'Don't give me any of your bloody cheek.'
Me: 'I'm not giving you cheek. I've gotta cold.'
Boss: 'Get off those drums. You're fired.'
Me: 'What!!'
Boss: 'You heard. You're fired. Get off the stand!'

The audience stared, in astonishment, wondering if this was some sort of cabaret routine we were doing. I slowly rose from the drum stool, picked up the sticks and brushes - which were my only possessions as a drummer - and awkwardly made my way to the side of the stage, climbed down ... and sat on one of the chairs which lined the walls. People looked at me, some of them laughing, some of them embarrassed, and most, like me, puzzled.

The boss turned to the band and shouted to one of the boys who played a saxophone, 'Danny, get on to those drums.' A second or two later he banged his heavy foot on the floor and shouted, 'a-one-two-three-four'. The band blurted out an untidy entry to the music of 'Jealousy', since they were as surprised as the dancers, but everybody soon settled into the beat of the tango except for my replacement drummer - who had just discovered that there were no sticks or brushes for him to use. He looked over at me but I just shrugged my shoulders, so he began making frantic signs, indicating his problems.

Then, suddenly, just as if somebody had blown their nose during a tango, the boss shouted 'STOP'! This time the reaction was half that of shock, and half a feeling of 'Oh, not again.' He turned to the drummer.

Boss: 'What's the matter?'

Danny: 'I've got no sticks to play with.'

Boss: 'What do you mean, no sticks?'

Danny: 'Val took them. They're his!'

The boss threw an ugly glance in my direction, 'Get back on those drums,' he said. A great hush fell on the place as I slowly climbed back on to the stage, shuffled my way behind the drums, and sat down. As I was about to look up in anticipation of the next move, there came the now familiar 'a-one-to-three-four'. We were off once again into the old routine. The dance went on until three o'clock, we packed-up, said goodnight, went home, and the matter was never mentioned again. To this day, I've never really known if, in fact, his tongue was in his cheek and that he was just sending me up.

After a six-month stint of one-night-stands, coupled with the fact that I was playing an instrument in which I had no interest whatever, I decided I wanted to move on. I still had very little to offer in the way of credentials, as far as a job was concerned, and had to agree with the boss when he tried to discourage me from leaving a steady income, while I had nothing else. It was Bruce, once again, who came up with a suggestion: each summer in a little seaside town called Bray, in County Wicklow, a small alfresco entertainment was presented on the minute bandstand on the promenade known locally as 'The Coons', after a kind of minstrel show they had there.

An area in front of the stage was railed off and used as an auditorium, where deckchairs were available at a small cost. Passers-by, of course, were free to stand by the rail and watch the show for nothing. For this reason the man who ran the show, a Mr Bolton, together with his wife, took turns in 'bottling' the crowd. (This simply means that between their brief appearances on stage, whether to sing, dance, or take part in sketches, they took a collecting box among those people who dared to stay even long enough to see what was going on.)

That was my next engagement! Between us Bruce and I played guitars, piano, sang duets, did comedy sketches with the comedian, compered and did anything else we were called upon to tackle.

For all that, and twice daily into the bargain, I got six pounds a week. I loved it though because, for the first time, I was doing the kind of thing I enjoyed and was my own boss. We had a lovely summer there and made lots of grand friends. I'm proud to say that, by the middle of the summer, the crowds were getting bigger, we were being asked for requests, and I think I felt the first flutter of excitement at being an 'entertainer'.

One evening I got a message saying we were wanted at the stage entrance (a tiny exit in the side of the little bandstand). Bruce and I went out to find a gentleman who told us his name was Niall Boden.

We were both somewhat flabbergasted, as this chap was

one of Irish radio's Terry Wogans of the time. He said how much he'd enjoyed our songs, guitar duets and so on, and wondered if we'd like to add a bass player, of our own choice, to the duo and form a group to do some radio work?

Needless to say we were thrilled and at once found a local player, named Kevin Whelan, who joined us on bass, thus forming the Bruce Clarke Trio.

Niall Boden was doing a fifteen-minute sponsored programme, twice a week, on Radio Eireann and asked us to do a trial show. The products being advertised were made by a company called Donnelly's; so we became the Donnelly Music Makers and spent our time singing the praises of sausages, ham and black puddings. We did this programme for about six months as far as I remember and, again, were fortunate to get very good public reaction. Being on the radio twice a week kept us in the public ear. Soon we found our services were being sought elsewhere and occasionally we augmented the group with a girl singer.

We taped the Donnelly Sponsored Programmes in an outside studio in Moore Street, a place best known as an open-air fruit and vegetable market. As you made your way to the Irish Recording Company, tucked away over one of the shops, you were entertained by a chorus of sales pitches all sung in the broadest of Dublin accents . . . 'Jaffe orangesss, Jaffe orangesss.' 'Nice fresh cauliflowersss, tuppence each.' 'Lovely bananas, five for sixpence.'

Bill Stapleton who owned the Irish Recording Company, was, by a strange twist of fate, that self same man who, with his mobile recording unit, had come to Waterford all those years previously, to put us 'on record' for the first time. He was a great friend to us both and not only gave his whole attention to the quality of our radio efforts but also allowed us to use one of his studios as a rehearsal room, when it wasn't otherwise required. To help keep the wolf from the door, Bruce and I started a little music school; he teaching the piano and me taking on young pupils who wanted to make a start on the guitar.

7   Change is just around the Corner

I hadn't been on the road very long before I discovered, the hard way, that the world is full of frustrated entertainers.

You just think about it. All you have to do, is visit your local pub, social club or dance hall, any weekend and, sooner or later, you'll come up against somebody who either wants to get up and sing with the band or play the drums or piano during the interval.

These people can be very insistent, too, especially when their courage has been boosted by a few stiff drinks.

Now it's a strange thing but I've found from experience that the singers with the greatest tendency to show off, are tenors. (I hope that all my friends in high places will know that they are exceptions.) Maybe it's the high notes that make them drunk with power, I don't know, but Ireland was certainly crawling with them in my early days.

I worked with one particular piano player, who had his own wicked method of dealing with these budding Mario Lanzas. Once he'd concluded that there was no way he could get rid of the volunteer vocalist, he'd say, 'All right, what do you want to sing then?'

'How about "Come Back to Sorrento"?' the happy newcomer would say, with 'partypiece' written all over his face.

'What key do you sing it in?' our friend Pat would ask.

'Oh! I don't know,' the tenor would admit, and proceed to sing a bit in 'la la la's'.

'Mmmm,' Pat would grunt, 'let's say, E minor. That should be OK.' He knew that the suggested key would take our friend to the limits of his range.

Once he had all this sorted out, he'd indicate the microphone to the singer and say, 'Right then, here we go, give it everything you've got, old son,' and proceed to play the introduction in G minor, a key that was guaranteed to give the poor man a double hernia before he got halfway through the song.

I was 'filling in' on drums in a band one night, back in the forties, when a very 'county' looking gentleman came clambering up on to the stand and headed in my direction. It was breaktime as it happened so there were just a few of us keeping things going while the rest had a beer.

'I say, old lad,' he said, 'could I have a bash at your drums? I used to play at university you know. Go on, there's a good chap.'

'Sorry,' I answered, 'we're playing for dancing right now and the bandleader wouldn't like it.'

'Oh! to hell with the bandleader,' he shouted impatiently. 'Let's have a bash!'

'Look,' I said, still playing, 'I'll be knocking off for something to eat in a minute, then it's up to you, OK? But do be careful.'

'Oh! you are a sport, old man,' he said, thumping me on the back and breathing beer and whisky fumes all over me and the drums.

He stood there, swaying from side to side, his hands buried in his pockets, till the set was over and then, eagerly, struggled into my drum seat. 'You know,' he whispered as I was leaving, 'I'm out on the town tonight. My horse won a big race here today and another of mine was placed in the Cambridgeshire, so – I'm in the money. When I've had a bash at your drums ... I'll give you a tenner for yourself ... how about that, eh? what?' I didn't believe a word and just headed for the tea bar.

When I got back he was finishing his attack on the poor drum kit and I could see, by his expression, that he'd enjoyed every second of it. The band began to set up for the second half.

'Thank you so much, old boy,' he shouted into my face. 'You're a good fellow. Now, I said I'd give you ten pounds and – here it is!' He thrust the ten pounds at me but no sooner did the thing appear in his hand than it disappeared into the hand of our bandleader, who smiled and said, 'That's kind of you, sir, it will go towards some new arrangements.' And he slipped it into his pocket. 'OK, lads, let's go,' he said, winking at us. 'That'll pay for all the booze tonight – I'm sure Val won't mind.' It was a genuine case of easy come, easy go!

I wondered at the time, with all the money the old gent had and his obvious love of the drums, why on earth he didn't buy a kit of his own. Still, he might have frightened the life out of his thoroughbred horses.

Within a year or so Bruce and I were regulars on radio, theatre and, of course, in dance bands, becoming more and more established in Dublin, both as partners, and individually. I personally found resident jobs quite a relief at times, since you had all day to 'do your thing' (as they say now adays), at the same time knowing you had the security of a regular weekly income.

The musicians in Dublin with whom I worked were a terrific crowd of fellows and, even though I will admit to being very much a loner, I did strike up some great friendships.

One of my mates was a drummer named Ronnie Leftwich who, like myself, lived on the south side of the city. We spent a lot of time together and his family extended the warmest hospitality to a wandering bachelor like myself; whenever I popped in there, I would share the results of his mum's culinary labours especially the cakes, scones and tarts.

Ronie surprised me one day by showing me a new purchase he'd just made. Standing by the kerb, right outside his front door, was a lovely little black car – a Fiat – the popular model of the time, that looked a bit like today's Volkswagen. He had been learning to drive and, as we were both working in the same dance hall at the time, wondered if I'd like a lift to work each night.

Naturally, I thought it was a great idea and immediately

joined him for a run round the blocks as a foretaste of the luxury in store. I'd never tried to drive a car myself, so Ronnie kindly agreed to pass on his newly acquired knowledge to me free of charge.

For a week or so there was a great crashing of gears and screeching of brakes to be heard in the vicinity of his house, while I struggled with the little machine. I got the hang of 'changing-up' without much trouble but found the reverse procedure of 'changing-down' quite a challenge. When in doubt I used to depress the clutch slow . . ly, apply the brake until the car was practically at a standstill, then start all over again. (In those days, incidentally, you didn't have to take any kind of driving test. You simply got yourself a driving licence and away you went.) With this very limited technique as my only qualification, one day I made the rash decision to go into Dublin City Centre to pick up some gear of mine left at a ballroom.

With my heart in my mouth and my fingers crossed, I set off on what turned out to be a most eventful journey. Because of my strange driving habits, I was tooted and beeped by one driver after another as I made my way towards the city and soon began to feel that I should have taken the bus. The whole disaster came to a head sometime later as I drove along a busy thoroughfare called Capel Street, heading for the bridge across the Liffey. As I reached the intersection of Capel Street and the Quay, the Guard on point duty held up his white baton directing me to halt.

In went the clutch, down went the brake, and I began to change the gearstick into neutral. Unfortunately, I didn't quite achieve my aim because, when I released the clutch again, the gears made the most sickening noise and the poor little car spluttered to a most undignified standstill.

The guard on traffic control looked scornfully at the cause of the awful noise, at the same time indicating that I should stay precisely where I was. Poor man, he needn't have worried as I was desperately trying to get the thing started again somehow but – without success. The long stream of traffic strung out behind me was headed by a green double-decker bus, the engine of which was belching out its impatience as the huge thing towered over the back of my tiny vehicle.

The inevitable happened and the Guard turned in my direction, his white stick smartly indicating immediate action. I couldn't move, he exaggerated the movement this time. I still sat there sweating, the cars behind showing their disapproval by honking in dozens of different keys – still nothing from the Fiat.

Almost dying with embarrassment, I looked into my mirror – only to see the drive of the bus throwing his hands up in frustration then, opening his door to climb out. I even thought about getting out and making a run for it but, too late, a big red set of knuckles banged on my window as the Guard on traffic duty gave up hope and decided to let the traffic – coming from the opposite direction – get on with it.

Sheepishly, I let my window down to be greeted by the booming voice of the bus driver, 'For Jasus' sake, son, will ya put that thing in ya pocket and go home!' he bellowed angrily in my face.

'I'm sorry,' I said, 'it's just stopped and won't go again.'

He looked up to heaven, slapping his hands against his sides, 'Get out,' he shouted. 'Let me do it.'

Feeling as though the whole world's attention was focused on me and my problem, I climbed out on to the road and my seat was immediately taken by the bus driver. 'You've flooded the damn thing with petrol,' he growled, 'we'll have to wait a minute or two.'

The couple of minutes that followed seemed interminable, passers-by gathering round thinking there had been an accident and the occupants of the bus peering through the window muttering all sorts of complaints which, thankfully, I couldn't hear. The eventual starting-up of the engine was like sweet music to my ears. Thank heavens the bus driver had mellowed a bit too, feeling, I'm sure, like a golfer who sees a colleague in the long grass, he probably thought, 'There but for the grace of God!'

'Thanks a lot' I said. 'Sorry for all the trouble.'

He smiled to make me feel better, 'Don't worry, son,' he answered, 'it could happen to a bishop!' As if I were a bishop, I offered up a little prayer that I wouldn't go and repeat my folly by stalling the thing again. Slowly I moved away half expecting a round of applause from everybody concerned – not least, the poor policeman who just stood there shaking his head.

One of the bandleaders I worked for quite a lot in Dublin was Bob Murphy. Bob was a good musician who played trumpet, led a very successful band but, in the main, was to find his forte as an arranger. We 'gigged' all over the place during the years I was associated with him and a good time was had by all. One job that sticks out in my recollections of his band, was an evening at the Town Hall in Dun Loaghaire, the busy channel ferry terminal outside Dublin.

He had a problem booking all the right guys for the job and, as a last resort, had to fall back on one particular musician reputed to be unreliable because of his taste for the 'bevvy'. 'If we can only keep him out of the bar, we'll be OK,' said Bobby, as we made the journey along the coast road towards the evening's venue.

But one thing he didn't reckon on, was that our saxophonist friend might get to a bar before the dance even began at eight o'clock. It was a beautiful evening when we arrived at the Town Hall of this attractive seaside town and we began to set-up on stage, chatting to each other and getting up-to-date with the latest gossip. Eventually, the man of the moment arrived and, as he walked up the hall, I heard Bobby whisper, 'Janey Mac... I don't believe it ... he's bevvied already!'

I'd never had the pleasure of meeting the gentleman in question and simply shook hands with him as he prepared his instrument for our tuning-up interlude. From that moment, we all got on with our job and I didn't give him another thought.

I think I've mentioned before but one of the things we

did in those days was to 'stagger' the band a bit – different groups having their refreshments at different times so assuring the patrons of non-stop dancing music right through the evening. Bobby sent me for an early break, while he led a small group of the boys in a kind of 'dixieland' session. Shortly after I got back, he prepared for another reshuffle; turning to our sax-playing friend he said, 'I'll leave you with Val on guitar and Ronnie on drums. OK? Just do some slow waltzes, we'll be back shortly.' Bobby left the stand and I looked across for some sort of clue as to what was going to happen.

My new partner donned his sax and approached the microphone looking, to my amazement, a bit the worse for wear.

'What'll we play?' I asked, looking up.

'Ah! mmm . . . slow waltz, isn't it . . . Ah! . . . how about "For you" in three flats?' he suggested.

My electric guitar amplifier turned up, I played a four bars introduction in E flat and off we went. A mike was conveniently placed near me, so I sang a vocal chorus in the middle, 'I will gather stars out of the blue, for you, for you,' and so on. The whole thing was fine and when it ended we acknowledged our applause.

Again I looked up, awaiting my instructions, 'Ah!' he said, looking a bit glassy-eyed, '"Ramona", in G, OK?' I plonked out four bars in G and was just beginning to think what a piece of cake it was when, to my astonishment, he actually played *For you* again – in *E Flat!!* I did a lightning modulation into his key, looking horrified as, indeed, did the dancers, who were no doubt wondering what was so special about the tune that we should play it again. Rather self-consciously, I sang the song for a second time and longed for it to finish. The applause was, as you can imagine, a bit grudging this time and I hoped we could just get on with things to cover the feeling of embarrassment.

Quite unmoved by it all, however, our featured soloist adjusted his sax-reed, looked across, '"THE ANNIVERSARY

104

WALTZ" IN C!' he shouted. At the end of my four bars introduction I hovered between the two keys, wondering what he would decide to do this time and – you've probably guessed it – he played 'For You' in E Flat. He'd obviously got some kind of mental block and couldn't get the one song out of his head – or his fingers. There was a groan from the dancers who looked up with 'Oh! For God's sake,' written all over their faces, as from the door of the refreshment room came our boss who obviously couldn't believe his ears. This time, when we reached the vocal chorus, I just refused to co-operate, deliberately changed key and sang 'The Anniversary Waltz'. This brought a little relief to the situation and, to round things off, my friend even consented to play a chorus of it to finish.

The band returned to their seats highly amused by the incident and, when Bobby announced a quickstep, I was waiting for some wise guy to suggest 'For You' in E Flat. The guilty party, on the other hand, sat serenely in his chair, apparently oblivious to his crime and probably thinking that he had, in fact, played three different tunes.

I was in my early twenties by now and quite accustomed to living my life in digs. Since Dublin was only about a hundred miles from Waterford, I made the trip to see my family and friends as often as I could.

It was hard to get used to the change in No. 10. It was so quiet with only my mother and brother Lar living there. Ned, Nellie and Una were married and living in their own homes, John was working in London and, as I mentioned earlier, Nancy was in America.

Strangely enough, it was during these visits that I really began to know Lar, having more time to talk to him over meals, or sitting by the fire at nights.

His health had been a constant worry to the family for as long as I could remember, and it was getting steadily worse.

It all began many years earlier when he got a tubercular

abscess in his neck glands. It was removed by surgery, only to be followed by another some time later.

Sadly, worse was to follow, and in time the dreaded disease got to his lungs. All kinds of medical steps were taken, culminating in a long period of rest at one of the country's leading convalescent homes.

But it was all in vain and the lung had to be removed.

After that, he was never fit or strong enough to take on any kind of heavy work, as the strain would have been too much for his heart. Eventually, he found himself a job doing some light duties at a local market garden and nursery, and seemed very contented.

During one of my visits, sometime around the end of 1949, he asked me if I'd like to go along to a local dance that evening, just to keep him company. I'd never been much of a one for dancing, but agreed to go just for the fun of it. During that evening, I became aware of how many times he had to sit and rest to get his second wind.

He told me the truth on our way home. We were climbing John's Hill which led to our house when he slowed down. 'I'll have to rest for a bit, boy,' he was breathing hard. 'I'm afraid I can't make this hill in one go any more.'

We sat on some stone steps leading to a terrace of houses and talked for a while. 'The doctors tell me the other lung is banjaxed now, and they don't think my heart can take the strain much longer. I could have a real bad haemorrhage at any time.'

There wasn't a lot I could say to help, 'You'll have to rest more, that's all,' I tried.

'Oh, I've accepted the situation now,' he went on. 'I only hope and pray that when it does come I'll be at home, and Please God in my own bed.'

I hadn't been long back in Dublin when I received a telegram from my brother Ned.

LAR PASSED AWAY SUDDENLY THIS MORNING. PLEASE COME HOME

I was on the next train from Kingsbridge Station in

Dublin, wondering what the news would be at home, and how my mother would be coping with it all.

Yes, he did have a haemorrhage, but God heard his prayers all right and waited till he was 'at home, and in his own bed'.

The shock of the whole thing, with the loneliness that followed, proved a great burden on my mother so, in order to give her a change of surroundings, I arranged for her to come to Dublin for a while.

If, by the way, you're beginning by now to come to the conclusion that there was a great dearth of romantic interest in my life, I've got to admit that you're not far wrong. Casual affairs with the opposite sex were never one of my strong points as a lad. That, coupled with the unfriendly hours my work inflicted on me, made my amorous encounters few and far between. I should also add that my enthusiasm for my work at the time was such that, given the choice, I'd probably practise my guitar rather than get involved with someone.

Looking back, I must admit that I missed out on a lot of fun in my early days. But then, who knows, if I'd been a different sort of fellow, I might have married and had three kids before I was twenty-five, made a lot of different decisions as a result – and ended up with no reason for writing this story anyway.

Life for me in the Dublin music world was, by now, a long succession of dance halls, radio shows, rehearsals for various things and, all in all, I was getting all the work I could handle.

However, they say that familiarity breeds all kinds of discontent and in time I was, to be perfectly frank, getting that feeling of having done it all before.

Towards the end of 1951, Bruce and I were both working in the resident band at the Olympic Ballroom in Dublin. (Ballrooms were a thriving industry at that time and, looking back, it's hard to believe that so many could find willing patrons night after night.)

One night as we were warming up and the hall was still empty, the manager came walking across the dance floor. 'Val,' he shouted over the tuning-up noises, 'can you pop down to my office for a minute, there's two chaps'd like a word with you.'

The two chaps in question were members of a vocal quartet called the Four Ramblers – an Irish group which was working in England, to which I listened with great interest on a weekly BBC radio show called 'Riders of the Range'. Their names were Pat Campbell and Dermot Buckley.

I discovered that a member of the quartet was about to leave, due to illness, and that the purpose of their trip to Dublin was to find a replacement. The qualifications were that he should be able to sing harmony lines, play guitar, do the vocal arrangements and, of course, try not to look ugly. After some initial enquiries, they were given my name by a fellow musician and now, having found me, they were offering me the job.

A change of musical surroundings was just what I needed at the time and, even though the offer contained very little in the way of guaranteed income, I had to say yes.

Within a month or so I'd said my farewells to Bruce, my staunch partner of so many years standing, been home to receive the blessings of my family and, with one suitcase and a guitar, was boarding the boat for England.

8   Across the Water

The boat train delivered me safely to London and into the hands of one of my new partners, who was there waiting to greet me at Paddington Station. Dermot Buckley, or Dee, as we all grew to call him, took me back to his bed-sitter for a hearty breakfast of bacon and eggs.

No. 20, Highbury Grange, London, N.12, became my world for a while. Dee had a room there as, in fact, did two other members of the group, who lived there with their wives. Our landlord 'Ossie' was a great guy, explaining that he sadly didn't have a room for me at the moment, but it was all right with him if I shared with Dee till something came along. He charged me £2 per week.

The boys were, as I've already mentioned, appearing in the BBC radio series 'Riders of the Range' written and produced by Charles Chilton, an exceptionally talented man. The programme described life on one ranch in the American west; you could say it was a sort of 'Bonanza' idea, tied together with music and songs. That's where we came in – we were the ranch hands, or bunkhouse boys, who happened to sing in the style of the Sons of the Pioneers from the old Roy Rogers, Gene Autry days.

Well, twenty-four hours after my arrival in London found me, pencil and manuscript in hand, writing the music for our first two or three vocal contributions to the radio show. I remember the feeling of excitement when I first heard the music I had written coming to life, with a group whose vocal style was so familiar to my ear from radio and records. We did the 'Riders of the Range' programme for about thirteen weeks and I found the new experience very thrilling.

That first three-month period also included my

introduction to the British Music Hall stage. I learned the 'Ramblers' established stage act and, glad to say, made a few suggestions of my own which, in time, were incorporated to good effect. We appeared for 'weeks' (one week at a time) at all the major towns and cities all over the British Isles during the next year and, by the time 1952 was spent, I was a fully-fledged quarter of the quartet.

Maybe it's because I was brought up in the environment of a small community that I've always thought of London as a place where people work or where people 'have' to live because of their work. I still can't imagine it to be so many people's Home Town – a place they think of as 'their' personal place. Goodness knows, I've met and been friends with enough Londoners (including being married to one) to know just how completely wrong my impression can be. What I'm trying to say really, is that the sheer size of London makes it impossible for a lad from the country to imagine it as somebody's 'village'.

I made my debut on the British variety scene when it was still in pretty good shape. For as long as I can remember people have propounded the old cliché 'Variety is on the way out', but it certainly wasn't showing any signs of disappearing in those early days. Week in, week out, we would travel somewhere to join the cast of a different show, especially assembled for that one occasion.

Of the dozens of stars who topped those bills, some would fall into the category of older and well-established favourites – names like JIMMY JAMES, JEWELL AND WARRIS, JIMMY WHEELER and MAX WALL. Then there were the younger stars like, HARRY SECOMBE, MAX BYGRAVES, TERRY THOMAS, HARRY WORTH, ERIC SYKES and so on. But it was undoubtedly the age of the singer. Each Monday, a different name would grace the front of the theatre, as a result of the artist's record and radio popularity. There were scores of them: DAVID HUGHES, ALMA COGAN, GARY MILLER, LITA ROZA, ANNE SHELTON, DAVID WHITFIELD, EVE BOSWELL, JIMMY YOUNG, RUBY MURRAY, THE DEEP RIVER BOYS, THE BEVERLEY SISTERS,

MICHAEL HOLLIDAY, LEE LAWRENCE, JOAN REGAN, LESTER FERGU-
SON, and of course the visitors of that period: JOHNNY RAY,
GUY MITCHELL, BILLY DANIELS. The list could go on, and on,
and on.

We were with Lester Ferguson one week in Southport.
In the interval we popped across to the local for a snack
and a drink. As we stood by the bar, an old guy came up to
us looking a bit sloshed.

'Here,' he said, nudging us, 'are you from the theatre?'

'Yeah, that's right,' we answered, wondering what was
coming.

'And are you the stars?' he asked. 'I've never met a star.'

'Sorry, we can't oblige,' we admitted, 'Lester Ferguson
is the star of the show.'

He looked at us in astonishment. 'Lester Ferguson?' he
gasped, 'and what's he doing in the show, may I ask?'

'He's singin' of course,' we said. 'What else?'

There was a long pause, after which he came out with a
line that floored us. 'He's singin' now, is he? Well, that
bugger has cost me a small fortune.' Then waving his
finger at us, he said, 'Tell him what I said. I hope he can
sing better than he can ride a bloody horse. And walked
off. It took us several seconds to realise that he was
thinking of, the then very young, Lester Piggott, who had
obviously let him down at the bookies.

Being in the thick of the music hall world, one of the
things I quite naturally wanted to do, when I came to
London, was to visit the London Palladium. This proved
much easier than I expected. It was a time of very special
variety shows at this great theatre. Such stars as JIMMY
DURANTE, GUY MITCHELL, MAURICE CHEVALIER, JUDY GARLAND,
DANNY KAYE, would appear there for a week, their
engagement including two matinee performances: one on
Wednesday and one on Saturday.

I just couldn't believe my luck when my new partners
told me that being a member of an established act,
provided you could produce some proof of identity such as
your Equity Union card or a visiting card displaying the

111

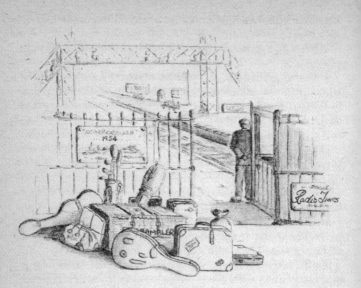

On tour with the Four Ramblers

name of your act, entitled you to free admission on the
Wednesday afternoon. So, the weeks when we were in
London would find us queueing, with hundreds of other
pro's, to watch the world's best entertainers in action.

What a treat it was. Time after time I sat there,
wondering what it must feel like to stand on that stage
starring in your own show. Never, in my wildest dreams,
did I think I'd see the day when it would happen for me,
not only for the odd week but for a six-month season!

One special area of employment being exploited by
London based agents around that time, involved travelling to Germany to perform in cabaret at the many clubs
on American Army and Air Force bases. An offer came our
way in the early part of 1953 and, work being a bit thin on
the ground at the time, we decided to have a crack at it.

Having sailed by cross-channel ferry to the Hook of
Holland, we boarded a Trans-European express which

travelled right across Germany; its final destination, as far as I recall, was Vienna.

After sitting up all night, drinking coffee and playing poker while the long snake-like train rumbled its way across the continent, we finally staggered out on to the platform at Weisbaden in the early hours of the morning.

Weisbaden was to be our headquarters for the duration of that four-week stay. (On other visits which were to follow through the years, we'd find ourselves stationed at locations such as, Stuttgart, Munich, Frankfurt or Heidelberg, taking in all the available venues in the respective areas. It was remarkable how such place names as Darmstadt, Manheim, Karlsruhe and Kaiserslautern became as familiar to us on the passing signposts as were Halifax, Tipperary or Leamington Spa.)

On reporting for duty next day we were surprised and somewhat shocked to discover the unfamiliar system of selecting and distributing the entertainment. Assembling at a large club, with dozens of other acts from Britain and the continent, we stood around rather self-consciously, wondering what it was all about and what was in store for us.

Entertainment officers from the many bases in the area gathered, with notebooks and pencils at the ready, while each act in turn went on stage and did their bit. At the end of this marathon audition, and when the buyers had made their decisions, they'd go into a huddle with the agent and book their shows for the coming weeks.

Then, depending on what sort of impression you made, the jobs were allocated. Some unfortunate acts got no bookings at all, others one or two. We, proudly, finished up with a very heavy schedule. Ironically, it didn't matter to us – as we'd been booked on a set weekly salary.

Then started a series of mystery-tours of Germany, doing one, two, or even three shows in one night and never before, or since, have I experienced such varied conditions and audience reactions. You could go to a base and do a show at the officers' club in conditions which were on a par with any first-class hotel, then go across to the place of entertainment set out for the enlisted men and be faced with the most horrific contrast.

One weekend we went to do an early evening performance at a place called Bitburg, which was situated just outside Nuremburg. We got there early and took a look around the city and were naturally intrigued to see the home of the famous Nuremberg Trials. It was still daylight when we got to the base and made our way to the N.C.O.'s club; we weren't too surprised to find the room practically deserted as the brilliant sunshine streamed in, reflecting on the cheap-looking chromium tables and chairs.

Now it was the accepted practice that these shows should run for at least fifty-five minutes, at the end of which time the officer in charge would sign a document stating 'the show was as booked' and all was well. If, for any reason, including being hit by flying beer cans, you didn't do the specified time, 'the man with the money' could possibly refuse to sign the chitty and no dollars would be forthcoming.

We started to set-up for the show. On one side of the stage stood a large TV set, about four feet high, worked on a closed circuit system which supplied the G.I. viewers with popular American light entertainment. On this occasion, the laughs were being supplied by the, then very topical, 'Amos and Andy Show'. As we walked about the place, making our initial investigations, our conversation was interrupted at intervals by shouts of, 'Ho, there, Sapphire!' or 'Holy mackerel, Andy . . . you don't say.' We brought our equipment from the car outside and began to cart it round to the back of the stage; I had a guitar in one hand and a very heavy amplifier in the other as I trundled through the swing door.

Looking round, I could see four people there: one fellow in fatigue dress, reading a paper and having a cup of coffee and a hamburger, a couple sitting on stools by the bar and another guy, in cowboy-style clothes, slouched in a chair with his feet stretched across the aisle and resting on an adjoining table.

I slowly approached the latter carrying my crippling baggage and paused, as I faced the barrier made by his outstretched legs. 'Ah! excuse me,' I said apologetically. The Lee Marvin-type character slowly stirred, tipped his hat from off his eyes, looked up and grunted, 'What didya say, man?' I thought my problem was obvious but smiled and went on, 'Sorry to bother you but I'd like to pass, please.'

He looked up at me, giving the impression that he always wanted to play this role that had just come his way, 'You ain't gonna pass here, boy,' he said, just like Lee Marvin would have done. 'Now, why don't you go raht back down there and come up the other sahd, OK?'

He looked at my luggage, 'Are you with the floorshow, man?' he enquired. 'Yes, that's right,' I said politely ... wanting to add, 'What the hell do you think I am, the milkman?' but, knowing he was twenty-five per cent of our audience at that moment, I didn't want to antagonise him. Then I added, 'I'd like to get to the stage.'

He looked at me for a long time, smiling through the cigarette smoke that covered his face, 'Well,' he said, 'let me tell you raht now, you ain't gonna make it, chicken, so, why don't you Git!'

Now of all the roles I've ever visualised myself playing, I must say, that that of picking a fight with Lee Marvin was the least likely, so, mumbling something under my breath, I lumbered through the tables to the other side of the room.

'Rude bastard,' I hissed.

'Holy mackerel, Andy,' said the TV!

Then came the next problem or problems; we couldn't find anybody to help us, there were no microphones to be found, no lighting – nothing! Pat, one of my partners, approached the barman, who was leaning on the bar, having a drink and watching the television.

'Pardon me,' he said, 'how do you do a floorshow here,

or who do you talk to about it?'

'Well, sir,' answered the barman with a welcome smile, 'you've gotta problem. You see, everybody's on manoeuvres right now. So, why don't you talk to Sergeant Gonsky – that's him, with the lady, at the end of the bar.'

'Thank you,' Pat said, grateful that somebody spoke to him, and approached the heavily built man in uniform with 'the lady'.

'Excuse me, Sergeant Gonsky.' He spun round slowly. (This one looked like Kojak with a crew-cut.)

'What can I do for you, Mac?' he asked.

Well, Pat told him all the things he could do and explained all the things we couldn't do.

He listened while sipping his rum and coke and, when my partner had finished, he said, 'Oh! well, I guess there's a mike out back somewhere, you won't need lights, there's nobody here – but, I think you'd better do the show just the same. OK?' We couldn't believe it, as we set about the task of looking for the mikes, but we finally got things working sufficiently to make it look as though we were doing the show.

The act before us played the accordian and got the most dreadful reception from the TV viewers, who found him a painful distraction.

When we started, things got worse. The TV programme had now changed to 'The Jack Benny Show' and we just couldn't compete. 'Lee Marvin' told us to shut up, then turned the television up to its full volume. Unfortunately, he could still – though barely – hear us, so, calmly, but deliberately, he rose, walked round the back of the stage and – pulled out the mike plug from the socket!

Believe it or not, we battled on, without being audible, until the magic fifty-five minutes was achieved.

Our job completed, we quickly packed-up and hurried from the place, hoping that Sergeant Gonsky had signed our 'release'. The laugh that lives on in my memory was that, as we left and I was struggling through the tables with my bags, a voice from the other side of the room – and

116

I couldn't but appreciate it – said: 'I told you, you wouldn't make it, chicken,' ... he was so right, we certainly didn't make it – chicken!

We certainly did make it on ninety per cent of the shows we undertook on the American bases. In the majority of cases, we were well treated by everybody in charge of the club entertainments, and the servicemen enjoyed the shows and showed their appreciation in no uncertain manner. The whole business of performing for people's pleasure tends to be like most other things in life – you take it as the norm to go on, do the show and everybody's happy. When you get a stinker, you remember it for a long time!

Whenever the pro's got together, over a drink in one of the German bars, you'd hear the normal stories of how they 'tore-em-up' at such and such a base; 'couldn't get off the stage' at so and so; 'did four encores' at this place or that – all this was treated with knowing nods, of the kind extended to anglers who caught one 'that big'. When the stories of horror began, the atmosphere changed and a good laugh was had by all.

We kept hearing about one particular base where the airmen's club had a reputation, second only to that of the concentration camps during the war. It was affectionately known as The Snake Pit for the simple reason that it was downstairs in a kind of cellar and the only entrance and exit was by means of a small staircase at one end of the large room. We finally joined the band of artistes faced with the challenge of The Snake Pit and set out with two other acts: a couple of girl dancers and an American, rope-spinning, storyteller. It was a very cold day, I recall, as we arrived at Rhein Maine Air Base where the infamous place was situated.

In spite of our impressions of the place and what we had learned to expect from the stories we'd heard, we couldn't help feeling that it would probably turn out to be just another night's work. As was customary, we got there early and prepared the staging of our acts. (By the way, we

117

worked on all these shows with just piano accompaniment which, by present day standards, makes one shudder.) We left our clothes and stuff in our dressing-room, which we were sharing with the other acts on the bill, and took advantage of the waiting time by having something to eat and drink.

I don't know if you've seen the film *Bad Day at Blackrock* starring Spencer Tracy – if not, forget it . . . if you have, the next part of my story will certainly ring a bell.

We stood in a line at the self-service canteen and had a look at the board which informed us what was available. I was a bit fed-up with hamburgers and french fries, so I decided to try the chilli soup and crackers. I ordered some from a coloured man in a snow-white chef's outfit serving behind the stainless steel counter, its display cabinet loaded with goodies.

In five or six seconds flat, my bowl of soup with a small packet of crackers was spun on to the counter top.

'Thank you, sir.'

'Coffee?' asked the black man in the white suit.

'Oh! yes, please,' I said, fumbling for some money in preparation for the cash desk a few feet ahead.

At that moment a large black hand appeared from behind me, holding one of those red plastic tomatoes containing ketchup.

As the big brown fingers gave the soft red ball an almighty squeeze, a resounding squelch heralded a huge dollop of red tomato ketchup into my chilli soup and a voice from over my shoulder said, 'Give it some flavour, man.'

I turned round to find a fellow, who must have been Muhammad Ali's dad, huge in build with a smile from ear to ear.

'That's clever,' I said. 'Do you do it a lot?'

He was enjoying himself, 'No, I don't,' he said, 'but, you know I've enjoyed it so much, I think I'll do it again,' and with these words, my soup received its second squirt of flavouring.

To my great relief I didn't have to do, what Spencer Tracy did to Ernest Borgnine in *Bad Days at Blackrock*, and give him a smart karate chop round the neck; I don't think I could have reached his neck, without climbing up on the counter, anyway.

I felt a firm hand on my left arm. On turning round I faced the Master at Arms in his smart blue uniform with a gun slung ominously from his belt, 'Will you follow me, please, sir?' he asked politely, and led me towards my dressing-room.

When we were out of earshot of the serving area and its clatter, he spoke again, 'Sorry about that, I'll have some soup and crackers sent to your room. The boys are a bit uptight at the moment, because its near the time for some of them to go home!' He sat me down in my room and, in no time, a waitress brought me my food 'on the house'.

An hour or so after that incident saw the club filling up with, what looked to me like, extremely young men and their lady friends. We fellows strolled to the bar for a drink, to give the girls a chance to get ready for the show and, by the time we got back, the place was packed.

It was time to go and do our stuff; the patrons were seated and the dance floor was raised into its new position as a cabaret platform – about level with the shoulders of those adjacent to the stage. And, as ever, they were knocking back beer from cans which had two drinking holes pierced in the top – these, to us, were always a hazard and replaced the 'rotten eggs and tomatoes' of the traditional music-hall days.

The technique used to attack any artiste who didn't please them, was to put their fingers over the holes in the top of the can, shake it furiously until it was ready to explode and then spin it along the floor in the direction of their victim. It resulted in – not being struck by a flying can, but it certainly assured some work for your local dry-cleaners, removing beer stains from your trousers. Over the years we developed great agility at ducking the froth, without missing a note.

The two girls went on first to do their dance spot, also

showing great dexterity at avoiding, rude, groping hands as they danced by. They came back to the dressing-room thoroughly annoyed and depressed by their reception vowing, as we entertainers so often do, that they would 'never go through that again!'

Not very encouraging for our rope-spinning friend who was on next. Well – he spun his ropes, told his stories and died the most humiliating death. I must give him credit, though, he did his time and 'kindly didn't leave the stage'. (This was something the final act desperately hoped for because any time cut by the first acts, had to be made up at the end – to satisfy the fifty-five minute rule.)

He staggered back to the room like an injured dog to his kennel, and dropped into a chair. 'Well,' he puffed, 'you're welcome to forty minutes of that bunch, gentlemen,' and slowly began to tidy up his ropes.

We waited for our introduction, heard the piano plonk out our opening music and, like four youngsters taking their first plunge from the high-diving board, walked on – smiling! The noise in the place was deafening. Our first two songs went without any reaction; we knew it would indeed be a long forty minutes that evening. It was about twenty minutes into the act when the first beer can came spinning from the edge of the stage and, ten minutes later, there must have been sixteen or eighteen of them surrounding our eight beer-splattered legs.

The real trouble came when one G.I., feeling dissatisfied with the effect of the ammunition used so far, decided to go for the 'big guns'; he used a can which still contained two-thirds of its capacity and assured himself, and us, of a spectacular climax.

He gave it a good shake, struggling to keep his fingers over the sizzling holes in the can – in fact, he had got up such a good head of steam that, as he tried to flick the can in our direction, it slipped – spun off at an angle of thirty degrees – overshot the other side of the stage and caught a fellow G.I. right on the nose! The old cliché 'all hell broke loose' is about the best description I can find for what followed.

The fellow with the bruised nose threw the beer can directly at the culprit sitting oppposite; his reaction was to climb on to the stage, walk across and leap headlong on top of his new-found enemy. Soon their buddies decided to help and before you could say, 'Two beers, please,' the scene was just like the saloon brawl in a John Wayne film.

We stayed as long as we dared to but, finally, decided that money wasn't everything and dashed for our room. I can't remember just how long the punch-up lasted but when the military police sorted it out, we were escorted from the club by my good friend the Master at Arms.

It was like heaven, coming out into the cold night air – safe and sound.

From there we headed for the offiers' mess to do another show and made some immediate enquiries about having the beer dried from our stage suits. Everybody was utterly charming and offered us something to eat and drink, while our suits were being pressed.

The gentleman in charge of entertainment, came and introduced himself as 'Major something or other'.

'I hear you had an unhappy time across at the airmens' club,' he said, smiling.

'Have you ever been over there?' we enquired, thinking it was rather a silly question.

'No,' he said, 'but I hear it can be kinda rough, at times.'

'Kinda rough?' we echoed in astonishment and proceeded to tell him of our night's ordeal. When we finished, we asked, 'Why is it allowed to go on?'

'Well,' he drawled, 'it's like this, I guess. The guys are anxious to get on back home and they're feeling a bit aggressive about it so, we reckon, if they're gonna loose their cool and hit somebody, it's best they hit each other and not the Germans.' I'm sure there is a lot to be said in favour of this philosophy but, from our point of view, it was like inviting somebody to your house for dinner and then spending the evening belting hell out of your wife.

Our 1953 trip to Germany, nevertheless, turned out to be the first of many visits undertaken in the fifties. We learned to cope with every eventuality and, in time, overcame the fear of the unknown which dogged our early ventures.

Another overseas trip that the group did, around that time, was a month's cabaret at a place called The National Scala in Copenhagen, Denmark. It was a large restaurant, near the Tivoli Gardens, which had nightly cabaret to the accompaniment of a good-sized orchestra.

We also doubled at the Night Club which was on the roof of the same building – it was much more a place for young people, who danced and had a few drinks.

The group that played up there was quite brilliant; a sextet of very talented Swedes who swopped instruments for different numbers in their repertoire. They also sang well together as a group and their arrangements were very much in the style of the, then, extremely popular, 'Four Freshmen'.

One beautiful moment in our association with them happened on our final evening at the club. The leader of the band, Paul by name, introduced us and said how sad they were that we were leaving . . . we did our act and left the stage to an absolute ovation. When we were about to return to our dressing-room, Paul brought us back on stage and asked us to sit in the audience, 'Because,' he explained, 'we have a little surprise for you, as a going-away memento.'

We made our way to a table near the stage, which had been tactfully vacated to accommodate us. The four 'vocal' boys then went off stage, announced 'The Four Ramblers', ran on again and absolutely staggered us – and the audience – by DOING OUR ACT. It was really sensational and the accuracy of their portrayals, of each one of us, was uncanny!

The day we arrived in Copenhagen we went straight to the National Scala and did our rehearsal. The stage manager informed us that we might have difficulty in finding accommodation, since there was some huge convention in the town. As it turned out, the word 'difficult' was a gross understatement and six o'clock that evening found us still searching without success.

Finally the stage manager rang a number and said to two of us, 'I've found you some place – it's not ideal, but it will do until tomorrow, OK?' We readily accepted, collected our cases from the dressing-room and set out to find it. Our instructions were to go over the bridge, past the cinema, turn down a small lane on the left, and about thirty yards on we'd find a green door. We were to ring the bell and say, 'National Scala.'

We rang the bell – a loudspeaker at the door-side said, 'Hello.'

We said, 'National Scala.'

A buzzer went, the door opened, and a flight of thickly carpeted stairs rose in front of us. We started to climb and were met by a fat lady who gabbled away in Danish and took us down a corridor to the last room, which was tiny, with two beds and a large tiled heating stove, of the circular type, with a chimney that went up through the ceiling in the middle of the room. We left our bags and headed back to do our show at the restaurant. I think we did OK, I can't remember much about the audience or our reception.

When the show was over, we went home – rang the bell – 'Hello' – 'National Scala' – up the stairs – the fat lady again – but now a great clamour of voices from all over the place, there seemed to be one big party going on. We went to bed shattered.

Suddenly, our door opened and the light came on. The fat lady standing in the doorway pointed to me and said, 'Telephone.'

'Me?' I said sleepily. 'Can't be, nobody knows me here.'

She pointed, harder this time, 'You, telephone – National Scala!'

I tumbled out of bed and, in dressing gown and slippers, followed her to her room where she had one of those funny phones on the wall like they had in Humphrey Bogart pictures.

I picked up the salt-cellar and bunged it to my ear, 'Hello, Val here,' and I waited for some awful broken English.

Instead, I heard, 'Hallo, mate, we can't find any place at all, can you help us?' it was the other two lads in our group.

I then struggled to ask the lady of the house if we could have two more fellows to stay. She smiled and said Yes, as if to say, 'if that's what turns you on' – only then did I know where we were staying and why everybody was having such a good time.

I immediately tried to tell her that my pals just wanted digs but she couldn't speak enough English to understand.

'Moment,' she said, putting a finger to her lips – and went away. In a moment she came back with a pretty girl of about nineteen, wearing a little see-through nightie. 'She speak English, she understand everything,' said the fat lady.

I'll bet she does, I thought as I reeled off our story.

She clarified the situation and I told the boys to come along and, hand in hand with 'baby doll', I walked back down the corridor. We parted, unfortunately, as we reached the first door where somebody was awaiting her return. I went back to bed.

A few minutes later, a knock at our door, and in came two men who proceeded to assemble two more beds in our tiny room. By now, the beds covered the whole room so, strictly speaking, the floor was two foot higher and we were sleeping on it!

Next morning we had four cups of black, evil-tasting coffee and left our 'hotel'. The fat lady said goodbye and no doubt thought we were the strangest customers she'd had in a long time. She'd certainly never run her trade with the likes of us: four fellows whose idea of a sexy night on the town was sleeping on the floor and drinking black coffee.

The hotel or 'pension', where we finally stayed, was very different from the kind of theatrical accommodation we were accustomed to back home.

It had many rooms, most of them occupied by pro's –

entertainers that is – of one kind or another, all of the tenants sharing one large kitchen. This was equipped with a row of about eight cookers, each one with an accompanying cupboard containing its supply of pots, pans, dishes and cutlery.

You simply brought your own food, cooked it at your leisure and even had the luxury of a lady who came to help with cleaning up after meals.

The pro's came in all shapes and sizes; the most memorable of them indeed, for shape and size, being an American double-act called Patterson & Jackson. (I'd seen these two coloured entertainers some time before, when they were appearing at the Prince of Wales Theatre, in London, in a show called 'Hellza-poppin'.)

The lift, or elevator, which served our third-floor hotel had a safety notice, which read, 'Maximum Load Three Persons' and, when I tell you, Patterson & Jackson had to travel one at a time, you'll not be surprised to hear they weighed twenty-five and twenty-six stones, respectively.

Warren Patterson loved to cook and spent a lot of his time in the kitchen. He was a real jolly soul and tap-danced about the place, in his dressing-gown and slippers, while preparing his enormous meals. He proudly informed us one morning that he had worked once as a chef and, to prove it, threatened to cook for us 'the best and most exotic Irish stew we'd ever tasted'. On his instructions, we bought the ingredients for this culinary treat and left them in a carrier bag on the kitchen table.

Next morning the ritual was scheduled to take place, so we all assembled in the kitchen eager to sit and watch an expert at work. Systematically the meat was chopped and the vegetables cleaned and sliced – all in a manner that seemed to prove, beyond any doubt, that this was to be no ordinary Irish Stew.

Warren swaggered about, from table to cooker, to the accompaniment of his non-stop scat-singing then, as the special brew finally got under way, he decided to enlighten us on one of the great secrets of cooking.

'You know what this is, man?' he asked, holding up a

125

clove of garlic between his chubby thumb and forefinger. 'Now lots of folks don't like the smell of it, right?'

'Right!' we answered in unison.

'Good,' he nodded, like a schoolmaster acknowledging the success of his pupils. 'You know somethin' else?' he went on. 'Some foods don't like the smell of it either so – what do they do? – they build up a resistance to it. Right?'

'Right!' we chanted once again.

'So! What do we cooks do about it? I'll tell you, man, you must take that food by surprise. See, don't let it know when that garlic is comin', right?'

'Right!' we shouted this time.

He was laughing by now and waving his piece of garlic in our faces, 'Now, here's how it's done.'

And this huge loveable man – the object of his strange demonstration now hidden in his clenched fist – began to jive about the kitchen then out into the hallway and back again, all the time singing some jazz chorus to himself.

Each time he passed the cooker, on which his prize dish was simmering, he simply smiled in the direction of the pot and sang a few special notes to it – as if trying to gain its confidence. On about the fifth circuit, and without any warning, he deftly popped the garlic into the bubbling stewpot.

'Got you, man,' he shouted. Stopping in his tracks and turning to us, he said, 'Now, there ain't no Irish stew in the world can live with that, man.' Then, flopping into an adjacent kitchen chair, he roared with laughter as, indeed, did we: like his clove of garlic he was quite irresistible.

Later we all sat round the kitchen table enjoying a most wonderful meal and agreeing that it was worth waiting for. Mind you, it tasted nothing like Irish stew!

My partner, Dee, fell in love with the cheese shops in Copenhagen. Unlike me, he's a 'smelly cheese' fan and tried hard to convert me to his outrageous tastes. Whenever he heard me coming, he'd hide his spoils from the local shop on the outside ledge of the window, so I wouldn't complain about the pong. I'm sure the poor pigeons in our district eventually classified our back yard as a 'disaster area' and decided to emigrate.

Working abroad is very good experience for any performer in my opinion, since it makes him prepare an act that has international appeal; the kind that will travel. Once you have worked abroad and found out, the hard way, all the things that don't work with a foreign audience, you are forced to expand your material in order to make it acceptable everywhere. This kind of professional 'investment' certainly pays off, by making your act saleable anywhere. How many times have we seen acts, that are fantastic in London or Scotland but, when they reverse their location, become a bit of a non-event.

9 Snakes and Ladders

We loved going back to Ireland.

The Theatre Royal in Dublin was a truly magnificent theatre to play with its huge auditorium, lots of dressing-room space and boasting a pit orchestra of up to twenty musicians which, by general standards in those days, was quite unique. Alas, like many other fine theatres, it has since been demolished.

We played there many times as you can well imagine, being an Irish act – on one occasion for a long session of several weeks. The show was a very extravagant and spectacular Christmas production which starred several of Ireland's leading entertainers together with some imported acts which, strangely enough, included ourselves.

As ever we were employed to take part in all sorts of scenes in the show but, in the main, we concentrated on our own spot. We shared a very large dressing-room with three or four other people in the cast and I'll always remember the fun we had together during the run of that particular show.

One of the people who didn't share our room was the star of a very well-established variety act of the period – a lady who went under the name of KARINGA. She was a most unusual speciality act, to say the least: accompanied by a couple of male assistants, she'd parade with great pomp on to the stage wearing a long cloak which trailed behind her and, when removed, revealed a tight-fitting, very slinky, leopard skin outfit which never failed to bring a few whistles from the lads.

She would then perform a series of feats – thrilling! shocking! scaring! but always entertaining her audience. First she introduced two huge alligators which immediately opened their mouths as if to devour the lady but, with the click of a finger and a few well-chosen words, she somehow hypnotised them on the spot. She then simply carried on with her act leaving the poor things lying there, right through its duration, looking like a couple of broken-down sports cars with their bonnets open!

She handled huge twenty-foot snakes, as you and I would the garden hose; then climbed a ladder, 'in her bare feet', the rungs of which were razor-sharp swords. (Their sharpness was naturally demonstrated beforehand by the cutting of pieces of paper, accompanied by the usual theatrical flourish, bringing gasps of approval from the youngsters.)

Finally, Karinga would lie on the stage and a huge slab of stone would be slowly lowered on to her prostrate body then, as she no doubt clenched her teeth in anticipation, her assistants would produce two enormous sledge-hammers and proceed to knock hell out of the slab until, eventually, it shattered into pieces round her body.

Slowly, she'd rise, then with a chord from the orchestra, she'd raise her hands on high and run forward to the front of the stage to tumultuous applause. This, she'd acknowledge by making that 'wanting to go to the loo' movement (a sort of semi-curtsey), with her shapely legs – in the style made famous by magician's assistants.

Now it was customary, after our afternoon show, to sit in our dressing-rooms with our feet up, with possible a game of poker going on, eating a light snack and having a cup of tea. Other members of the gang would slip through the stage door to the pub just across the road – for slightly stronger refreshments.

On this particular afternoon, I was sitting enjoying a pork pie and a cup of tea when an announcement came over our dressing-room speaker requesting the entire cast to assemble on stage in fifteen minutes' time. Pretty soon a great gathering of assorted folk wearing stage make-up, in dressing-gowns, hair curlers, some of them finishing their last mouthful of sandwich, littered the huge Theatre Royal stage.

The Manager appeared – everybody stared at him in eager anticipation. 'Ladies and gentlemen,' he began, 'if you'll give me your kind attention for just a few moments' – there wasn't a sound anyway – 'I don't want to cause any kind of panic and let me assure you, right away, that there is nothing to worry about but I regret to inform you that one of Miss Karinga's snakes seems to be missing.' There was a shocked silence.

The fellows looked at each other and one or two summed up the feelings of the others with such remarks, as, 'Bloody hell!' The girls, on the other hand, squeaked and pulled their dressing-gowns around their legs.

'Now the reptile must be somewhere in the theatre,' the Manager went on. 'A thorough search is being made, both front of the house and backstage, so I will ask you to do tonight's show just as you would any other performance and, remember, there is *no* danger; the snake is quite harmless!'

The meeting broke up and everybody made their way slowly back to their rooms looking about them anxiously. I don't think I need to tell you what it was like, eyes were everywhere and there seemed a natural tendency to stand quite still and not move anything or anywhere.

'Overture and beginners, please,' came as a kind of ice-breaker really, and pretty soon everyone was onstage, waiting for the opening music for our evening performance. Of course, all of us had different ideas as to where the snake might be. One of them suggested it could be in the pit which, after all, is where they are reputed to be found. This only caused the poor orchestra to play in a half-sitting, half-standing position all eveving – ready for take-off, as it were.

Ours really is a strange way of life, you know – I swear the 'Pagliacci' thing is absolutely true: as soon as we come in contact with the audience, all else is forgotten. Your private little world can be falling about your ears but you

130

must not let it show when you are on stage; and so it was with the cast of our Christmas show. There was a twenty-foot snake somewhere at hand, not having had his tea, slithering about getting more and more impatient with his lot, and there we were shouting to the innocent members of the public such gems as, 'Oh! yes there is!' to which they predictably replied, 'Oh! no there isn't!' Little did they know.

By the time our solo spot in the show came round things were in full swing and thoughts of our slimey friend were fading, at least temporarily. We sang our first two songs with great success and followed them with a very snappy comedy routine; next came our dramatic and most effective version of the old cowboy classic 'Cool, Clear, Water'.

The lights changed to a moody glow and the monotonous chanting of the word 'water' over and over again, filled the theatre with atmosphere. As we poured our hearts into this tragic story of a fellow dying of thirst in the American western desert, I became dismayed when I noticed several people nudging each other and sniggering in the first few rows.

To be honest, on such occasions, the seasoned pro's first reaction is to check if his flies are undone but, alas, the sniggering got worse until, pretty soon, the entire theatre was in hysterics.

We went on singing, 'Keep a movin', Dan – don't ya listen to him, Dan,' at the same time looking at each other for some kind of reassurance when, suddenly, one of our lads whispered aloud, 'Look behind ya!' Gingerly we turned around and there, believe it or not, dangling by his tail from a batten at the top of the back-cloth, his head wandering searchingly ... about three feet from the stage, was the snake!

We stood rooted to the spot while the audience continued to fall about laughing, thinking no doubt that it was part of the act. What on earth were we to do?

All at once the hubbub stopped and so did the orchestra

as, from the wings, wearing her great cloak, strode Karinga and, in a loud voice reminiscent of Zsa Zsa Gabor, shouted 'Gentlemen! s'cuse me, please, for just one moment.'

We stood, speechless, our backs to the microphone, eyes glued to our new-found partner – the snake.

It was to the latter that Karinga turned her attention next; grabbing him by the neck she gave a sharp pull and his long body whiplashed through the air to the stage. She then picked him up and wrapped him twice around her kneck, turned his towards her and looked him straight in the fangs: 'You naughty boy,' she snapped, 'you naughty, naughty boy,' at the same time smacking him on the nose with her spare hand. 'Where have you been? You scare the life out of everybody but, worst of all, you spoil the nice gentlemen's act.'

She waited, as though expecting him to apologise, but he said nothing, so she went on, 'Don't you ever do that again – never!' One last smack on the nose and then she turned to us, 'So sorry, boys – do carry on.' Well, I ask you . . . you try following that with an impression of the Ink Spots!

It was shortly after I joined the boys that I had my first introduction to golf and, I must say, it's something for which I will be eternally grateful.

A few years back I had the great joy of playing a game with the legendary Bing Crosby and I can't find better words to describe my love for this sport, than the ones casually voiced by the great man. 'You know,' he said, as we strolled down the beautiful eighteenth fairway at Gleneagles in Scotland, 'if I were to give all I have in the world to golf, I don't think I'd begin to repay it for the pleasure it's given me.' I can't say the quote is accurate but there was no doubt whatever about the sentiment.

Two of the Ramblers, Dee and Pat, were quite keen on a game and for my first try coaxed me to brave the course at Bellisle, just outside Ayr in Scotland. I hired some clubs

Learning to play golf in Scotland
1952–3

for half a crown, paid a further few shillings to play and, three hours later, I was hooked. Through the following years we played on a great variety of courses all over the British Isles.

Having had my first taste of the game I was quite convinced, as indeed every golfer is, that next day I'd do so much better. I felt that I knew what I was doing wrong and, given a little time to work it all out for myself, I'd soon come to terms with its elusive technique. With this in mind I decided that next day, weather permitting, I'd wander out to the course all on my own and, free from the distractions and embarrassment of being watched, discover the secret.

The following morning I hired the clubs, paid my green fee, and headed for the seclusion of the first tee, which was nicely hidden from the view of any of the people in the vicinity of the Clubhouse.

Having briefly refreshed my memory on the basic principles passed on to me by my colleagues on the previous morning, I teed up, selected my club and addressed the ball.

'Are you going to have a bash?' said a lovely rich Scottish voice behind me. Startled, I turned my head to find, approaching the tee, an elderly gentleman dressed in what I later learned was the typical uniform worn by many older members of clubs: a pair of grey flannel trousers, which had seen their best days, an old frayed waterproof jacket with a zip-fastener down the centre and, on his head, a tweed peaked cap.

Feeling very self-conscious, I walked away from the waiting ball and answered, 'Well, I was just going to play a few holes.'

'Good, good,' he said happily. 'I'll come round with you.'

I felt I really should either back out of the whole thing or, at least, explain that it was virtually my first time on a course. 'Oh! I should go ahead if I were you,' I urged him. 'I'm afraid I'm a complete novice and I'll only hold you up, please carry on.'

He wouldn't hear of it, 'Don't worry, son,' he assured me, 'everybody has to start some time. I'll help you along.' Then, stepping back as if to give me plenty of room, 'Go on, off you go, don't worry yourself.'

I stepped up to the ball, every nerve in my body tingling, desperately trying to resettle my thoughts sufficiently to remember what to do.

I hit it on its head as it were, sending it squirting over the top of the elevated teeing area. It landed on the fairway, just the other side of a tiny stream that ran at right angles to where I stood!

Well, if the effort had filled me with depression and frustration, it certainly had the reverse effect on my new-found friend. With a reassuring smile in my direction, he walked up to the spot I'd just vacated and casually prepared for his opening shot. And what a nice shot it was too, flying through the air, right on target, up the centre of the fairway.

From that moment on I was treated to a non-stop stream of golfing theory all of which, I'm sad to say, only increased my confusion. By the time we came to about the sixth hole, I'd heard the entire history of the man's golfing activities right from his schooldays, when he caddied for this fellow and that fellow, to this year when he had won several senior prizes.

I should say that he wasn't bragging but genuinely trying to stimulate my golfing appetite, give me confidence and improve my technique in any way possible.

We came to a very impressive-looking par five hole, some five hundred yards or more in length.

'Gosh,' I said, 'this is a long one!'

'You know something, son,' he replied, 'you think this is a long hole! Well, I'll tell you right now, I never take more than six shots on this hole.'

I was very impressed indeed as I scuttled my tee shot some sixty yards along the ground.

To my surprise, his stroke wasn't much better. 'Ach,' he grunted, picking up his bag and heading after his ball.

Some three shots later he was in a bunker about two hundred yards from the green. He hacked the ball out.

'Five,' I counted under my breath, 'he'll have to hole this out from one hundred and ninety-six yards to score six.' He took a rather casual swing which sent the ball into the rough, on the left-hand side of the fairway. I waited for his comments.

Quite unmoved, he strode over to the spot where the ball had entered, picked it up – and put it in his pocket. 'I never take more than six shots on this hole,' he said. I'll bet he had a few victims with that one, over the years.

Like many other touring acts in those days, we had no cars or any such luxury so we simply travelled to all our theatrical engagements by British Rail, having loaded our personal baggage, our stage props and music instruments plus, of course, three sets of rather battered old golf clubs, into the fishy-smelling guard's van.

When we played places like Newcastle, Swansea, Glasgow or Clacton-on-Sea, we made enquiries on our arrive as to the whereabouts of the local Municipal course – knowing that these courses, which were run by the Council, would be much less expensive than the private and more classy ones. We'd find the appropriate bus next morning and off we'd go for our three or four hours of bliss.

They were such happy times that I still can't visit those towns or indeed hear mention of those same courses, without the memories of my first games flooding back to my mind. Sometimes, the bus would drop us three-quarters of a mile from the golf course and we'd happily walk the rest of the way without flinching.

Dee was a very calm and most reliable member of the group, both socially and musically. It was he who met me on my arrival in London back in 1951 and, I'm pleased to say, he's still one of my closest friends. His golf, however, was not quite so calm and he looked upon the striking of the ball as quite a vigorous affair.

His greatest asset to me, though, has always been his sense of humour. We were having a game one day, over on the Isle of Man, with danceband leader, Bob Miller, who led the 'Millermen' on radio for so many years. Bob took his golf quite seriously and, in spite of playing a good game, was never quite satisfied with his efforts.

We'd reached the eleventh hole, which was skirted by the airport. Bob was not having too good a game on this occasion and was last to play off the tee. Dee prepared to play his shot, 'Ah! you see, lads, the idea is, emulate the masters,' he said in his impish Barry Fitzgerald style. 'Right now I'm thinking of Ben Hogan,' and with these words, he hit a superb shot down the fairway and smugly walked back to his bag lying on the ground.

'Right,' I said, as I waggled the club behind my ball, 'relax now, Val boy – think of – oh! Perry Como,' my shot went straight down the middle.

It was Bob's turn now and his giant figure towered over the tiny white ball. 'Let me see,' he muttered, 'I'm going to think of Henry Cotton.' He took a magnificent swing at the ball but sent it, slicing away to the right, over the fence into the airport!

Sadly gazing after the little white dot, Dee enquired, 'What happened to ya, Bob. Are ya sure ya weren't thinkin' of "Billy Cotton"?' Bob collapsed into fits of laughter and went to his bag for another ball.

Right from the first day I joined the four boys, I got used to seeing bags of golf clubs lying about the theatre dressing-rooms. Like anybody else I was always tempted to slide one of the clubs out of its bag just to see how it felt.

'Don't swing the club indoors,' they used to say. 'You don't realise how long the thing is and you'll end up doing some damage.' Dee said, 'There are more lamp-shades in Britain broken by golf clubs than by Hitler's bombers.'

I stood in our dressing-room at the Empre Theatre, Middlesborough, back in 1952, a number seven iron in my hand. Slowly and carefully I swung the club back over my shoulder, watching its progress as it went and remembering my partner's advice. It seemed pretty safe to me so, confidently, I took a couple of smooth swings at the spot on the frayed carpet which I'd chosen as my imaginary ball.

'Nothing to it,' I thought to myself moving a little further to the right, just in case, my eyes glancing occasionally at the lampshade. Sad to say, I went a little too far to the right. My back-swing reached a very early climax on this occasion, and a horrible sound of splintering wood, accompanied by a strange, distorted musical chord, stopped me in my tracks. My natural reaction was to return the club to its address position, but my efforts to do so only resulted in revealing one of the most horrific sights I can ever remember. There, sus-pended on the end of my seven iron, looking like a salmon which had just been speared, was my partner's pride and joy – his beautiful handmade guitar which he'd left leaning against the wall. A cold sweat covered my face and, at that moment, I'd have given anything in the world to have been guilty of simply smashing a lampshade.

So, if you're just taking up golf, I can't give you better advice as a beginner than to say, 'Don't swing the club indoors!'

We worked a lot in Scotland throughout the fifties, doing seasons both long and short and finding that our set act, coupled with local type material, helped us no end to cope with the problem of having to change our programme every couple of weeks.

I was fully occupied night, noon and morning, during these engagements; not only doing the act, but also taking part in sketches and production scenes and preparing all the music for the following week's programme.

The first half of the show was usually closed by a musical 'scena' of some description, the producers drawing on many different sources, Scottish, Irish, French or American medleys or, maybe, a pot-pourri of melodies from the great musicals.

Once the choice had been made the appropriate costumes would be hired, as required, from a local theatrical costumier, arriving on Monday morning in time for the dress rehearsal. Everybody made a mad dash to the large 'skips', or baskets (once the principals were suitably rigged out), hoping to get the pick of the bunch and praying for a decent fit. I wasn't too badly off since I was fortunate enough to possess a reasonable set of measurements – something which didn't apply to some of my colleagues. Our bass singer, Dee, for example, was short in stature and invariably found that his sleeves and trouser legs needed hems of several inches before he dared enter the spotlight.

'The Merry Widow', we were told, was to be the first half finale one particular week, so we all set about learning the many melodies which involved our participation.

Our costumes turned out to be pink suits, white shirts

and black bow ties so, one at a time, we stood in front of the dressing-room mirror admiring or ridiculing our respective appearances, depending on how we had fared in the lucky dip. Sometimes a swopping session took place in the hope of some improvement but it rarely came to the rescue of our problem child, Dee.

Our tenor, a Welsh lad named Frank Davies, drew our attention to his shoes – the squeakiest footwear I've ever known – and it was suggested that he should restrict his movements on stage to those occasions when the music was at its loudest.

Frank, however, was not the kind to be easily subdued so we waited with bated breath on opening night. Halfway through the musical extravaganza, the soprano was to walk forward and offer her rendition of the beautiful melody 'Vehlia'; the four of us, together with other members of the chorus, tastefully scattered about the stage, as if we were enjoying a pleasant evening at the Ball.

The soprano began, 'There once was a Vehlia, the witch of the wood,' while we stood, champagne glasses in hand, 'Ooh-ing' and 'Ah-ing' the musical background. At the end of the verse, the music gradually decreased in tempo, culminating in a sort of pregnant pause – as if the whole song was taking a breath.

It was at this point that Frank gently swayed forward on to his toes, then back on his heels, getting the maximum effect from his squeaky shoes. The poor lady soloist flinched, hesitated for a second or two, before sallying forth into the chorus. 'Vehlia, Oh! Vehlia, the witch of the wood,' accompanied, this time, only by a couple of shaky voices, plus lots of sniggering and snorting, as the remainder of the cast tried desperately to contain their laughter.

For the rest of the week this spot in the show was dreaded by one and all – as everybody waited for Frank's sound effects.

The following week we treated the audience to our version of 'Rose Marie'. This time, my partners and I joined the Mounties – and what an assortment of Mounties we turned out to be! Dee finished up with a hat that was so big, it needed pages one, two, three and four of the *Daily Telegraph* tucked inside the rim to make it fit.

We spent most of our time in this particular production, marching about the stage and waving our fists threateningly at the audience, as we chanted, 'On through the hail – like a pack of hungry wolves on the trail. We are after you, dead or alive, we are out to get you, dead or alive,' Dee's hat, suspended above his head, looking more like an umbrella and giving the impression it could drop on to his shoulders at any moment, his head disappearing inside.

When the time came for the baritone and soprano to join forces for the familiar 'When I'm calling you-oo-ooo,' we discreetly retired to the wings to await our next entrance. We were to march on, in single file, crossing over a ramp at the back of the stage partly camouflaged by cardboard cut-outs of pine trees. On cue, we entered with our usual 'On through the hail, etc.,' our numbers swelled, this time, by two extra members of the cast in similar Mountie outfits. As we reached the opposite side of the stage we would dash madly round the back, only to enter once again, hopefully, giving the impression of a long stream of red-coats.

It might have worked too, if it hadn't been for Dee's hat ... there was no possible way the Royal Canadian Mounted Police could have issued one of those to every 'sixth' recruit!

When we were informed that our next undertaking would be a Dutch scene, we couldn't help wondering what on earth our contribution could be. The only obvious title that came to mind was 'Tulips from Amsterdam' so it came as no surprise when the song and its stage presentation went into production. All the dancers stood in line across the footlights, holding in front of them a variety of cut-outs shaped like tulips. These had been treated with luminous paint and at a specified time the stage was thrown into darkness and the Ultra Violet lights were switched on. This produced the stunning effect of a long row of multi-coloured flowers swaying in time with the music.

At the end of the song the tulips were passed from one girl to the next, gradually disappearing into the wings, where the waiting stagehand would pile them in the corner.

Things were fine until, one night, the stagehand wasn't there. The unfortunate girl at the end of the line stood in complete panic as the tulips, one after the other, were thrust into her arms. 'Will somebody take these bloody things,' she shouted, 'I can't hold on to them.' Finally, the whole lot went crashing to the floor, bringing one tribute to Holland to a most undignified end.

However, once the girls had made their exit, the spotlights, blazed on to the centre of the stage to discover four 'Dutchmen', hands clasped behind their backs, strolling towards the footlights in time for the old song, 'The Jolly Brothers'.

When we reached the microphone we had, believe it or not, to whistle the thing. Now whistling on stage can be a highly dangerous and risky business at the best of times and, what with the collapsing tulips and squeaky boots, the producer, after one or two performances, had second thoughts ... and suggested we 'la la' it instead.

Before leaving the subject of production scenes and costumes, I should mention that our greatest problems occured in 'Scots Week'. You see, this always meant that, a pound to a penny, we'd be wearing kilts. Dressing in this garment is not to be taken lightly in Scotland as, understandably, they're very fussy that you should do the thing properly. However, the kilts arrived in such a variety of shapes and sizes that it was almost impossible to look anything but ridiculous. Poor old Dee ended up one week with a huge kilt tucked-up under his arms and secured to his shoulders by a tiny pair of schoolboy's braces! If any true Scotsman in the auditorium had known of such blasphemy, I'm sure we'd all four have been deported.

10 The Lady of the Amp

If entertaining happens to be your chosen way of life, one thing is pretty certain: you are destined to travel – and travel a lot! Your journeys may not take you far afield but, the chances are, they will be varied and frequent. My memories of towns tend to fall into the same pattern as those of golf courses I've visited; the better my 'score' the more pleasant my mental picture of the place is likely to be.

I've got wonderful memories of certain places which may not have the glamour, for example, of San Francisco, Rome or Mexico City. I'm talking of towns like South Shields, Ayr in Scotland or Great Yarmouth, simply because my first visits to those places worked out well and that's how I've continued to remember them. On the other hand, Exeter, which undoubtedly is a lovely place and where I made some great friends, brings a strange chill to my bones.

Way back in the mid-fifties the boys and I did a pantomime there and, for some strange reason, I found it almost impossible to find any decent digs. For the first week or two I just moved from one place to another, only to find myself leaping from 'frying pan to fire' on each occasion.

Since, at that time, I had a small bachelor pad in London and no family in England to spend my Christmas with, I decided to brave the holiday in my digs and be on the spot for our opening matinee on Boxing Day. I told my current landlady of my intentions and assured her I wouldn't be any trouble or impose on the family get-together in any way. 'Please yourself,' she said. 'but I'll be up to my eyes.' Well, I planned to drop a few hints around and maybe be invited to spend Christmas day with somebody in the show.

Alas, as I left the theatre on Christmas Eve, it looked as though I was sentenced to a day in my bedsitter with the gasfire full on and a generous supply of shillings neatly piled on the meter in the corner. Like a good boy, I got up and went to church on Christmas Day and – if you think that was a sacrifice – you only have to think of the alternative: a longer day in my room! I wandered back to my digs along the frosty streets and felt that, as I was on 'full board', I could at least look forward to a hearty nosh in the afternoon. Needless to say there was no telly, or anything like that, so it was down to 'Family Favourites' on the radio and a last run-through my part for tomorrow's show.

At about one o'clock, there was a gentle tap on my door and the landlady popped her head round the corner, 'Ah! s'cuse me, love – I'll be going out shortly, so would you like something to eat now? I won't be back till early evening.' She just stood there, half in the room and half in the hallway, and awaited my eager, 'Oh! yes, thanks. I'll eat now if that's OK.' The door clicked shut and she pattered off to the kitchen where the rest of the family were making lots of lovely Christmas noises. I cleared my table … and waited.

It seemed an age before the 'yoohoo' outside the door announced the big moment. I rushed to open it, knowing her hands would be occupied with the loaded tray. 'Here you are,' she said proudly, 'I've done you a bit of bacon and egg, a pot of tea and a couple of mince pies. Just leave the tray in the kitchen when you finish. I'll be off out now.'

'Bye,' I said and sat down … to what I think was the longest day of my life!

Next day at the theatre, just as I expected, I was inundated with belated invitations. 'Oh! you should have come to us,' or 'We thought you'd be off to London, what a shame.' Yes, it was a shame – I'm better organized these days, mind you!

In recent years I've spent a couple of very happy seasons in the nearby holiday town, Torquay, and, as I've driven along the Exeter by-pass on numerous occasions, I've smiled quietly to myself and can practically smell the bacon and egg wafting through my memory.

Considering all the hundreds of wonderful digs we had through the years, it really shows how strange human nature is, when the bad digs are always the ones you remember.

I'll give you a rundown on one or two memorable ones:

There was Liverpool, where the landlady ushered me into a sordid little room with a flag-stoned floor, an old iron bed, a plain wooden table, and in the corner an ancient kitchen sink that was absolutely filthy. On the Monday night, my supper was served in my room and the landlady went off to bed.

An hour or so later, as I lay there trying to sleep, I began to hear all sorts of scratching and scraping sounds coming from the other side of the room. Switching on my bedside lamp, I discovered several families of mice helping themselves to the remains of my meal.

Next morning, I complained to the landlady, and showed her the butter dish. 'Look', I said, 'you can see the droppings and footprints all over the butter.'

She held the dish closer to her face, her eyes screwing up behind her thick glasses, 'Oh, yes', she whimpered. 'So you can.' Then, picking up a dirty knife, she calmly scraped the butter into a fresh cube and placed it back on the table, disposing of the scrapings on the side of the plate. 'Now then,' she said, as she headed for the door, 'will a bit of bacon be all right for your breakfast?'

Then there was Leeds where I was given what was obviously the children's room, with toys all over the place and Donald Duck wallpaper partly hanging off the wall. Halfway through the night, the bedroom light suddenly went on and I sat bolt upright in bed. Framed in the open door was a huge lady in a voluminous nightdress, sloshed out of her mind.

'Who the hell are you?' she screamed. There wasn't much point in telling her who I was at that stage. 'What are you doing in the children's room, you cheeky begger,' she shouted, as she proceeded to tear the bedclothes off me.

When I did offer some resistance, at the same trying to explain why I was there, she stormed out of the room crying out, 'Will somebody come in here, there's a man in the children's bed.'

Next thing I heard was a man's voice trying to calm her down. A minute later, a gentle hand switched off my light and slowly closed my door. 'Sorry about that, son,' said the man's voice. 'Sleep well.' I never did discover who the woman was.

There was a parrot in our digs in Newcastle one time, who chatted away happily to all and sundry. His party piece, however, was as follows: Every now and then, he'd make a noise for all the world like a man whistling for his dog. Quick as a flash, a big black shaggy dog would come charging through the door and stand in the middle of the room, looking around in amazement, as if to say, 'Did somebody call me?' The parrot, on the other hand, would simply shrug his shoulders, sway gently from one leg to the other, repeating over and over again, 'Silly bugger ... silly bugger ... '

I never could understand how the dog kept on falling for the gag time and time again. But then, it was theatrical digs, and maybe it was all part of a well-rehearsed double act, especially laid on for the guests.

We had lovely digs in Blackpool on one occasion. The only other guest apart from a continental acrobat named Bob, and myself, was a charming spinster lady who worked as a schoolteacher at a local school. We saw very little of her since our hours varied so much and we ate at different times.

One of the acts on the bill that week was a musical duo called WOODS and JARRETT. Charlie Woods was a slim agile

145

man, who tap danced and sang. His partner, Bertie Jarrett, was a giant of a man who played piano, sang, and supplied most of the comedy in the act. They were both black, by the way.

One night, during the week, Bertie invited some of us around to his digs to sample his food and drink although I had to decline his kind offer, as I had quite a bit of music to finish for the following morning. However, Bob, the acrobat accepted, saying he'd see me later, and assuring me that he had a key for the front door.

Next morning I sat down to breakfast at the usual time.

'Where's Bob?' said the landlady, 'is he having a lie in?'

I said that I doubted it, since he was a very athletic gentleman and liked to get up early.

'I'll give him a shout,' I told her.

Popping my head round the corner of his door, I discovered that his bed had not been slept in.

'He didn't come home,' I reported, as I returned to the dining-room.

'Oh yes, he did,' replied the landlady, raising her eyebrows in a knowing kind of way, 'and his steps were very heavy on the stairs too.'

'Well,' I said, getting down to my breakfast, 'he must have gone out again. I hope he didn't disturb the school-mistress.'

'He couldn't have done that,' assured the cook, putting some fresh toast on the table. 'She went home to see her mother last night."

Quietly, I left the table and slipped upstairs, heading straight for the schoolteacher's room. There, sleeping like a baby in the spinster's bed, was our continental friend Bob.

The story unfolded at the theatre that evening. It seems that Bob, who was not used to drinking, had had far too much wine and passed out. Bertie decided to carry him home on his shoulders, had found the key in his pocket, opened the front door, carried him upstairs (hence the heavy footsteps referred to by the landlady), opened the

146

first door he saw, discovered an empty bed, unloaded his passenger on to it, and left.

Can you imagine the situation, had the schoolmistress *not* gone to see her mother. At four in the morning she'd have woken up to find a six foot four negro standing in the room with a continental acrobat on his back – the mind boggles.

Staying in different digs, and sleeping in different beds, can create all kinds of problems for somebody who takes more than a few drinks, as I'm sure people like commercial travellers would agree. You imagine waking up in the middle of the night, slightly the worst for wear. First of all, you can't remember what town you're in, much less remember, as you lie there in the pitch darkness of a strange bedroom, what the geography of the house is, and how to go about finding the bathroom.

This situation was a constant threat to a certain musician I once toured with on one-night stands.

One fateful night, after a heavy drinking session, he woke up, wishing that the bathroom was very close at hand. I was in another of three single beds in the same room, and heard his fumbling efforts as he tried to decide which side of the bed he should emerge from.

After stubbing his toe a few times, and letting out a couple of agonised cries, he seemed to find his goal. I heard the clicking sound of a door opening, and was about to settle back to sleep, when there followed even louder fumbling and moaning noises. It was time to come to his rescue so, climbing out of bed, I headed for the only light switch in the room, which was by the door.

The sight which greeted me when the light came on, caused me to fall on to the nearest bed with roars of laughter. There was our poor friend, in a desperate state of urgency, clambering his way out of the built in wardrobe with the jacket of somebody's best suit draped over his shoulders.

There's one hair-raising 'town memory' of mine that dates back to February 1953; the town was Bedford. The boys and I were working in a show run by the comedy duo Morris & Cowley and were doing a week at the local theatre there, which was known as The County. Our duties with this travelling company including appearing in the opening and the finale, taking part as required in sketches, cross-overs, or any other production and, of course, doing our act 'proper' to close the first half.

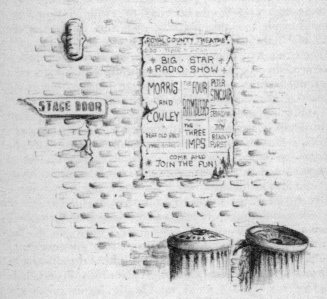

Variety bills in the early 1950s

At one point in the show, it was arranged that I made a special entrance as follows:

Harry Morris and Frank Cowley are doing a patter-spot at the microphone, centre stage. On a given cue, I enter from the wings, upstage right, wearing a mackintosh, trilby hat, horn-rimmed spectacles and carrying a

148

suitcase. I walk diagonally down the stage and leave by means of some steps situated in the lefthand corner. I then walk along the front row mumbling the occasional, 'Pardon me,' as I step over people's feet, continue to walk smartly up the centre gangway and leave the theatre through the front of the house.

Harry and Frank stand and watch this in mock amazement. As I finally disappear through the exit doors, Harry says: 'Who was he?' and Frank replies, 'I forgot to tell you – this is a short cut to the station!' This interruption was one of many that took place during their conversation and, like the old 'I say, I say' routine, was very funny.

Now, as it happened, their double spot was immediately followed by the Four Ramblers singing a song and because of this the timing of my little 'walk-on' was critical. I just had time to run round the front of the theatre, down the alleyway by the side of the building and through the stage door. As I appeared backstage the boys would cue our intro by running on stage, clicking their fingers in tempo. I would then throw off my mackintosh, hat, glasses, don my guitar and rush on to join them, just in time to start the song which was with 'just' four voices with guitar and rhythm accompaniment. If I happened to be a few seconds late, the boys simply repeated the intro once more.

Over a period of several weeks we learned to time the thing to perfection. We did so in Bedford – on Monday, Tuesday, Wednesday, Thursday ... but ... Friday ... tragedy!

On cue I made my entrance, walked downstage to the stalls and out through the front doors into the cold, drizzly, February evening. (Once outside, I'd learned to unbutton my coat and remove my glasses, to save precious seconds when I returned backstage.) As I began to undo my coat, a hand grabbed my arm and a drunken voice shouted, 'Hey, you! Is the show any good. eh?'

'Yes, great show,' I said desperately, trying to pull myself free from his grasp.

149

'Good is it?' he asked. 'Then why the hell are you coming out?'

'Look,' I shouted, 'I'm in a hurry, let go!'

Instead of releasing my arm, he grabbed my other arm with his free hand. 'In a hurry are you?' Then, looking at the case, he laughed, 'Have you robbed a bank or something?'

By now I knew that my partners would be getting desperate in the wings wondering where I'd got to, 'Let go!' I shouted furiously and swung myself away from him. He went flying as I made a mad dash down the alleyway towards the stage door.

Unfortunately, in my panic, I lost my balance, tripped off the pavement and went sprawling along the cobblestones on my face and hands. Then, as I tried to regain my balance, I twisted my ankle. I lay there for a few seconds in the mud and rain, wondering what on earth I was going to do. Eventually, I staggered through the stage door where my anxiously awaited return was greeted with a voice shouting, 'He's here!' Before I could say a word the three boys were on stage, clicking their fingers like mad, keeping an eye on the wings in anticipation of my appearance.

Little did they know that as they clicked away I was, in fact, being helped to my dressing-room to have my sprained ankle attended to.

When the lads eventually crowded into our room, I looked up 'Sorry, fellas,' I said, 'you must have been mystified out there, wondering what was happening.'

One of the boys laughed, 'Not half as mystified as the audience,' he chuckled. 'After all, it's not often you see three fellows come on stage, click their fingers for a minute and then – run off again!'

While we were appearing for a week in Sheffield, I bought a new guitar amplifier and, as we didn't possess a car and travelled everywhere by train, I thought it wise to make a soft leather cover, with a reinforced front section to protect the loudspeaker.

Going on the scrounge backstage, I asked the stage manager if he could help. He took me snooping around the prop room and soon found a large display board made from some kind of plywood. 'How about this?' he enquired. 'The leather will cover it up and it's quite strong.

I was very pleased and went about marking and cutting out a section about twenty-four inches by eighteen. The job done, I turned it round to admire the result and there, framed in my handiwork, was a picture of a very beautiful lady.

The caption read THE LOVELY LYNNETTE RAE AS ROBINSON CRUSOE. When I looked at the bit I'd thrown away, it read: CAPTAIN AND MATE played by MORECAMBE AND WISE. Sorry, lads!

Lynnette Rae was a most successful leading lady, with a great singing voice and two of the shapeliest legs in the business; and it became a standing joke from then on that, each night, I tucked her safely away inside my guitar amplifier.

One Sunday afternoon, a year or so later, we sat quietly in our digs browsing through the Sunday papers and waiting for teatime. A folded newspaper plopped into my lap. 'There's an article in there about your girl friend in the amplifier,' Dee said, as he got up to stoke the fire.

I thumbed through the pages and found a tragic account of how this popular singing star had suddenly lost her voice while appearing in a famous show of the period: THE FIVE PAST EIGHT SHOW, a regular presentation at THE ALHAMBRA THEATRE, GLASGOW.

She had developed a cancerous nodule on her vocal chords which meant that, for a period of three years, she was not allowed to sing a note and, for twelve months of that time, not even allowed to speak. She had to walk about carrying a note-pad and pencil as her only means of communication. When, at the end of that time, the medical experts felt that the vocal chords were sufficiently rested and strengthened, the next vital step was taken. The

151

affected area was cauterised after the surgeons had warned the patient that there was no knowing to what extent the voice would be affected, or altered. Luckily for her, the operation was a complete success although, as was feared, the top register of her voice was no longer true.

But there was no stopping the lady. In a short while, and in spite of a greatly reduced salary, she was back on stage using all her past experience and skill as an artiste to sell her newly acquired singing voice.

I handed the newspaper back to Dee, and winked my approval: 'You see,' I boasted, 'I don't put just anybody in my amplifier. I know a winner when I see one.'

The fact was, I had never laid eyes on the lady – well, at least, not yet.

One of the great hazards of being in a vocal group is the difficulty of keeping the fellas together. Unless you are very fortunate, the chances are you will lose a member through either domestic problems or his ambition to make it alone. So many guys in groups find that there is pressure from their wives or girl friends because of all the travelling involved and, unless the partner is very tolerant, he'll be nagged with the inevitable, 'Oh! you're not going away again,' or, 'How long will you be away this time?'

The only thing that makes solo work any different, is that invariably the rewards are greater: you don't have to share the salary, not to mention the fact that you get personal recognition – which you don't as one of a group.

During the period I spent as one of the group, I think we had about nine different people as members at various times. Again, when I was the subject of *This Is Your Life*, I was faced with them all at once and felt a bit as if I'd been a member of a large male-voice choir.

I stayed with the boys for eight to nine years and enjoyed the work very much. Being with them prepared me for things to come in a way that I never anticipated. Learning to write music freely, reading vocal parts at sight, planning the running order of a stage act, singing harmony with other people, accompanying others on guitar, and, most of all, learning to accept the fact that there are other people involved who may feel very differently about things from you; all are invaluable to me now in making my television programmes.

As the fifties neared their end, the time was slowly but surely approaching when I felt I should make some kind of fresh move in my career; I honestly thought that the group had about come to the end of the line. Just then, we were asked to join a concert tour with Anthony Newley. Tony had made a couple of very successful British musical films and, within months, was topping the charts with one hit record after another: songs like 'Do You Mind,' 'Personality' and 'Pop Goes The Weasel.'

The tour was a sell-out, opening at the Palace Theatre in Manchester. Travelling up there by train, we took our usual taxi drive to the stage door. Passing the front of the house, all four of us almost yelled in unison: 'HEY, LOOK AT THE BILLS.'

There, across the middle of the colourful posters, we read: 'The Glamorous Singing Star . . . LYNNETTE RAE'. Inside, I saw her for the first time as she stood on stage taking her rehearsal, wearing a white trouser suit and looking suntanned from a recent tour of the Far East. She really looked worthy of anybody's amplifier.

Our greetings were brief, Mr Newley doing the honours. At that particular moment, in fact, she was much more concerned about some bass parts which were missing from her music. 'I'm sure Val would do them for you,' one of my partners offered.

Within minutes I was scribbling out substitute parts, for which she was grateful, kindly offering to brew us some coffee in her dressing-room. We'd made a friend.

Later in the week Tony announced that the next day was his birthday and a celebration was to take place at a local club which he'd hired for the evening.

I had just taken delivery of my very first car, a brand new bright red, Austin A40, which had cost me £650. There it was, proudly ticking over outside the stage door, as I prepared to leave for the party.

Miss Rae appeared through the stage door. 'What's keeping my taxi, Albert?' she asked the doorkeeper.

'Don't know, Miss Rae, I ordered it ages ago,' he answered 'They must be extra busy tonight.'

I put my window down, 'Would you like a lift, Lynn?' I offered.

I gave her a lift to the party – about the best move I ever made. A couple of years later, we were married.

Funnily enough, it was at that party that another big decision in my life was made. One of the light-hearted items on the agenda was that all the artistes in Tony's show had to get on the stage and do some sort of solo performance – their normal stage acts weren't allowed. Singers did impressions, dancers sang, musicians did magic and so on. Since I was a member of a singing group, I was forced to part company with my three partners and try to go it alone.

Frankly, it didn't present too much of a problem for me: I simply got a Spanish guitar, sat on a stool and sang a little Irish Folk Song – nobody in the company had ever seen me do this before so, it came as quite a surprise to them.

My offering went down very well, not least with Tony Newley, who later spoke to me over a drink, 'Have you ever thought of doing that kind of thing on television and radio?' he said.

'Oh! not really,' I answered. 'Mind you, I used to do it in Ireland years ago so it's nothing new to me.'

'Well,' said Tony, 'I think you've got something there, singing the songs, explaining what they are and so on. I'd give it some thought if I were you, you won't want to stay in the group forever!'

That's what prompted me quite soon afterwards to ask for a BBC audition. Funnily enough, I didn't see Tony ever again after the show finished, but in 1973 my show followed his into the Prince of Wales Theatre, in London,

154

for a season. When I arrived in my dressing-room I found a note on the mirror, 'Hi, Val, who'd have thought you'd be following me into this dressing-room. Love to Lynn.'

As I write, I've just completed my 1979 television series during which one of my special guests was Anthony Newley. We sang a medley of his hits from the late fifties – fate had travelled a complete circle.

Luckily, I hadn't neglected my solo interests throughout my membership of the 'Ramblers'. Quite early on, in fact, just after 'Riders of the Range', Charles Chilton wrote a musical documentary called 'The Story of the Texas Cowboy'. It told the story of the West right through its history and, in so doing, explained how the cowboy came into existence. It was illustrated with songs of the West, from Round-up songs to Rebel songs and from Railroad songs to Campfire songs. This programme starred Tex Ritter the American Cowboy Star and he, together with Charles Chilton, did the research in the area of music and songs.

I got a very nice job quite apart from singing and writing for the quartet. Charles told me that Tex knew hundreds of old traditional songs but had no music for them; my job was to go with Charles to Tex's hotel room, discuss the songs then, when Tex found a suitable one, he'd sing it through and I'd write it down as he sang it.

For some strange reason, Tex insisted on calling me 'Cal' and refused to accept the fact that it was wrong. Some nights we worked till all hours and got nowhere; he'd choose a song, sing it, I'd write it down – he'd sing a different version, I'd write that down too – he'd then say, 'I like the older version myself, but I can't think of it right now, so forget that one for the moment.'

This went on for hours and I finished up with a dozen songs, none of which we were going to use. If my face showed any sign of frustration, or worry, Tex would smile and say, 'Now, Cal, don't you go gettin' all het up about these derned songs. They're only songs, boy. They'll still be there when we're all dead and gone!'

I must say that I always enjoyed Tex's sense of humour. He was willing to adopt his 'movie cowboy image' at exactly the right moments and did so – to great effect and to everybody's amusement. Wearing his natty western-style suit, high-heeled boots and stetson hat, he walked out of the front doors of Broadcasting House in London one afternoon, while I walked behind carrying my guitar case and a bundle of music. We'd just been doing some pre-recording and were heading for BBC's Aeolian Hall, in New Bond Street, for a further planning meeting with Charles, in preparation for the following week.

The 'Irish' Cowboy
The radio series with Tex Ritter, 1957

Tex hailed a passing taxi, which pulled in to pick us up at the kerb. 'Where to, guv?' the driver said, leaning out of his window. 'Can you take us to Aeolian Hall in Bond Street?' asked Tex, as the taxi driver smiled in recognition.

'With pleasure, sir,' he answered.

'Tell me, driver,' requested Tex, almost confidentially, resting his arm on the roof of the cab, 'how much are you going to charge for this service?'

'Oh! about two and six, sir,' replied the surprised driver.

Shaking his head, as though stunned by this outrageous cost, Tex turned to me, 'I sure wish I'd brought my horse, Cal,' he said, smiling all over his face.

That evening, after a long stint of musical research, Tex decided he wanted a late meal. Picking up the phone in his hotel room, he rang the number of his favourite Italian restaurant. 'Hallo, Mama,' he shouted, 'this is Tex. Me and my friends want something to eat,' there was a pause. 'What do you mean, closed? Well you can darn well open-up again, 'cause we're on our way.' He put the phone down and picked up his hat.

He got a royal welcome at the restaurant, where a special table had been prepared. I sat fascinated while he and Charles discussed, in great detail, the history of the American West – a subject very dear to both of them.

The proprietress brought the menus and Tex ordered his favourite dish. I just gazed at some of the chef's offerings, as a friend of mine would say, 'like a crow looking into a bottle!'

'Are you having trouble with that menu, boy?' shouted Tex, slapping me on the shoulder.

'I'm trying to find something I've heard of,' I said, laughing.

Before I could say another word, Tex's rich western drawl rang out across the room, 'Can somebody kindly bring an IRISH MENU, for this boy here.'

Good job the place was empty!

Later, as we sipped our coffee, Tex asked me about my name – Doonican. I told him that, on enquiry, I had discovered I was the only one in Ireland and I'd traced the name back some seven hundred years – he was truly flabbergasted by the idea of anything going back so far. Charles said, 'When we leave here, Tex, I'll show you something really old.'

We got in the car and Charles drove to London's St Pancras Church. It was now 3.30 in the morning and we stood at the gates, gazing at the ancient building surrounded by gravestones and trees.

'That was built about the year 600,' said Charles.

Tex gasped, 'Six hundred?' he whispered quietly. 'God dammit, I never knew there was anything that old.'

We kept looking.

'You see that old stone seat there, under the trees?' asked Charles. 'Well, that's where the poet Shelley used to sit and work.'

We waited for Tex's reaction. After a long pause, it came. 'Shelley eh? ... Hmmm ... Well you know somethin', I can quite believe that he worked among the tombstones ... 'cause dammit, that guy sure wrote some mighty dry poetry.'

Charles's next venture that was of interest to us was a musical picture of the American Civil War. He called this one 'The Blue And The Grey'. It turned out to be of extra special value to me personally, as he kindly booked me to do three solo numbers with the orchestra. This was, as it happened, my first solo appearance on British Radio and the first time I was to hear my own name announced rather than the group.

I used to sing with the guitar quite a lot, just for the fun of it and to keep my hand in. Thanks to 'The Blue And The Grey', I began to ponder over the possibility that, maybe, there was a future in it for me.

Now in my early thirties, I was living in a nice little bachelor pad, in a block of flats on the south-east side of London. One of my partners, Pat, also had an apartment in the same block – where he lived for years with his wife Oona and their children. Quite a bit of the act's rehearsing was done at our respective places, where we would perfect our intended contributions to such engagements of the period as, 'Workers Playtine' or 'Midday Music Hall'.

My friend Harry Morris and his family lived in Peckham, not far away, so I managed to visit them a couple of times a week. As I said before, Harry was very interested in my career and encouraged me to write for interviews, and auditions, whenever he thought the occasion was right for me. It was Harry who contacted the then BBC producer, Richard Afton, requesting an audition to appear in one of his many shows. The result of his efforts brought the offer of an interview, which I was delighted to accept.

I was instructed to go along to a church hall in the Shepherds Bush area where Richard Afton was rehearsing and, on arrival, was told that he would see me as soon as he found a few minutes to spare. I sat and watched the rehearsal for what seemed like hours until, at last, they broke for tea. The cast were sitting around in groups, chatting and having some refreshments, when I received the message that he was ready to see me.

Richard, cigar in hand, as ever, beckoned me to come up to the top of the room then, with my foot resting on an old chair and the guitar perched on my knee, I sang one song after another. When I finished he just looked at me, smiled and said, 'Good ... very good. I'll give you a TV spot all right,' and before I had time to acknowledge his kind offer, he added, 'as a matter of fact ... I'll give you several spots.' And he did!

He was presenting a show called 'Beauty Box' at the time – it was a women's magazine type show, with beauty and fashion interests. I was to be the musical interlude which was my first experience as a television entertainer. The orchestra on the show was conducted by Alan Ainsworth and the arranger was Ken Thorne – a man who was to be another of the guardian angels in my life.

11 A Sight of the Crock of Gold

There's nothing like a fruitful audition to drive you on to further efforts so, with the taste of success in my mouth, I moved again.

I wrote to BBC radio requesting an audition which, to my surprise, was immediately granted and soon I was making my way to Broadcasting House guitar in hand and ready for action. This time I stood in an empty studio, facing a BBC mircophone, while the people who were to judge my efforts sat in another studio – neither party had the faintest idea what the other looked like.

I sang a little American folk song, next 'Delaney's Donkey', then 'Scarlet Ribbons'. Again I was passed as fit for radio, and told that, when the right slot came along, they would contact me. Pretty soon a letter arrived, informing me that they had something that might fit the bill and suggesting that I should go and speak to the producer. It appeared that the 'Woman's Hour' programme was off the air for a short summer recess and the BBC were preparing all kinds of alternative ideas to fill the time slot: one of the suggestions was that a selection of solo artistes should do fifteen minute shows, each one making his, or her, contribution on a specific day.

I sat at home and worked on my 'Wednesday' spots; I finally decided to write short stories which would be linked together with songs. The idea worked well and led to more and more radio for Val Doonican including some vocal spots with the Frank Chacksfield Orchestra on Sunday afternoons.

I then did something that took the nerve of old Nick and, even now, I feel a slight twinge of embarrassment when I think about it. I wrote to the man who, at the time, was Head of Light Music at the BBC asking if I could have an interview (it was a bit like going to see the managing director of a large industry, looking for a job on the assembly line) feeling quite sure I'd be passed on to a producer. However, to my great surprise and pleasure, the interview was granted.

Mr Baines was seated behind his desk, my letter in front of him, when I came into his office. He told me to take a seat. 'Now then, what can I do for you, Mr Doonican?' he said, looking very friendly. He must have thought me quite naïve when I began my story, the sole message of which was that I was looking for work – just like anybody else.

'Well,' I began, 'I'm with a vocal group at the moment. You see, it's pretty steady living, and even though I want to work on my own now, I'm worried about leaving the group till I have a sort of stepping stone.' I paused for a few seconds, then went on, 'What I really need is a series of radio shows to make the move worthwhile.'

He looked at me for a few seconds, an expression of surprise on his face, no doubt thinking to himself, 'Well, at least the lad's got nerve,' then, picking up my letter, he said, 'According to this, you've been doing some solo work on radio so, let's just say that I'll make some enquiries, and then, we'll see what we can do.'

He pushed his chair back and stood up, so did I. Having thanked him very much, I left.

A few weeks later, I was somewhat shattered to receive a letter from the BBC offering me an engagement as resident singer on a proposed series of light music shows called 'Dreamy Afternoon'. It was to take the form of thirteen half-hour shows, consisting of light orchestra items played by Sidney Bright and his music, interspersed with songs from yours truly. Some of my contributions were to be performed with guitar accompaniment, others with the orchestra.

Some of the songs I sang were unusual, to say the least, and needed an explanatory announcement. So after a week or two, the producer suggested that it might be a good idea if I performed this duty myself. After a bit of a shaky beginning, I got used to it and, in time, enjoyed it. By the time the series came to an end, my little bits of chat had become quite an acceptable and important part of the show.

This fact became very clear when I received a letter telling me that the show was returning for another series and this time, it was suggested, I should introduce the entire show. I accepted the offer, and the name of the programme was changed to 'Your Date With Val'.

So, from singing the odd song, my duties had now been extended to writing and introducing the show, reading out letters and requests and even welcoming the occasional guest. For all that, I received the sum of eight guineas. This was however one time when the old adage 'Money isn't everything' applied in no uncertain manner. That series, which was to run for some hundred and twenty shows, changed my life. I shall never forget its producer, James Dufour, now retired, without whose encouragement and advice I'd never have found the same success on radio.

One little anecdote connected with those shows is , I think, worth relating. Before starting on 'Your Date With Val', I thought it a good idea to write a special signature tune. Having done so, I scored it for three guitars, went to a recording studio, and recorded all three parts – the finished product was most effective.

On the fateful day when it was to 'take to the air', the recorded signature tune was dispatched to the studio. Alas, somebody goofed and the vital piece of tape went to the wrong studio, away on the other side of London.

'It might get here on time,' said Jummy Dufour. 'In the meantime, can you just whistle it through with your guitar, just for timing.' This I did. When transmission time came around, the elusive tape had still not been located. 'Sorry, old lad,' said Jimmy, 'you'll just have to whistle some more.' I did so, on the air, everybody seemed to like it, and that's how it stayed. The tape hasn't arrived yet!

Working on my own was a very comfortable feeling to me. I'm not suggesting there was any strain with the boys, quite the opposite, in fact, but there is always the restrictive possibility in a group of having every decision vetoed from four angles. The comfort came from the complete freedom of being your own judge of what to do and how to do it.

Slowly, but with great care and forethought, I began to piece my new solo career together. I had my radio show now and hoped I could do it well enough to be asked to continue with it but, I also knew, I'd have to extend my work in other directions, as the radio show paid very poorly.

My producer, James Dufour, was aware, at the time, that I had been befriended by one of the country's top arrangers Ken Thorne (who you may remember did the 'Beauty Box' TV show) and was having private tuition from him in orchestral arranging. At home I'd sit in my then unfurnished spare-room with an old piano doing arranging exercises in the form of orchestral scores of various tunes, each one for different instrumental groups. I'd arrange, for instance, 'Somewhere Over The Rainbow' for a small group of strings and rhythm, then do it again for a small jazz group and so on. These scores I would take across to Ken's house in North London.

First we'd have a game of golf together and then, after a light snack, retire to his music studio where he'd go through my work step by step. He explained, however, that the only way I'd learn to know if my arrangements really worked was to hear them played, so my next move was to do something about that.

It was customary in those days that if you sang a song which was on the 'plug list', in a radio or television show the publishers would, in most cases, supply you with a special arrangement. If the score had to be done by a freelance writer, rather than a staff arranger employed by

163

Scoring at last
Orchestral arranging for BBC radio, 1960-1

the publisher, then a fee of about eight guineas would be paid for his service. The BBC, on the other hand, had to foot the bill for the lesser-known songs or, at least, the ones that were no longer hot property from the pop charts. Based on this existing situation, it was agreed that both the BBC and most of the publishers would pay the fee direct to me if I did the scores and, incidentally, write out all the orchestral parts as well.

From then on I planned well ahead and did a couple of scores every week, always taking them to Ken who cast his expert eye over them before they were finally commited to orchestral parts.

The whole thing worked like a dream for me and, pretty soon, I was turning out scores quite rapidly – with less and less disastrous results. Ken filled me with confidence and his patience and kindness played a very big part in my early success. He was, in fact, to arrange and conduct the music for several of my television shows and recordings in later years. The result of my initial arranging efforts changed the fee for my radio show, from eight guineas overall, to sixty pounds or more. The work was very hard and time-consuming but then, it's difficult to achieve worthwhile results in any other way.

Incidentally, the reason the programmes were called 'Your Date With Val', was that most people were absolutely convinced that nobody would ever remember the name 'Doonican' and so it would be best ignored. Therefore, for two years, I had no surname as far as the radio listeners were concerned. I was either 'that Irish fella who sings on such and such a morning' or 'that Val bloke on the radio'.

Housewives wrote and said. 'What's your proper name?' 'What do you look like?' and so on. I read these letters out over the air and asked them to guess but never made them any the wiser. Their efforts at describing me were great fun – most of them thought I was an old bearded guy like Burl Ives since, as they explained, young singers wouldn't do 'Delaney's Donkey', 'Paddy McGinty's Goat', or old songs like that!

Fortunately, the shows went down great with a lot of people and, pretty soon, I was asked to show myself in cabaret – mainly at functions organised by people who enjoyed the radio programmes. Things were now beginning to happen: I'd learned a lot from the listeners' letters, which I read with great interest and the overall opinion was that I was down to earth, uncomplicated and, as most people put it, 'ordinary'. I hope I still am!

I didn't have an agent at that time, nor did I really need one as my entire work was virtually wrapped up in music and the radio show.

Then one morning I had a call from an agent whom I knew through the Ramblers and who booked many acts for the US Bases in Britain. Most of these places would have floor shows on a couple of nights a week and acts were constantly heading out of London in mini-buses, or cars, to such destinations as Chicksands, Bentwaters, Lakenheath, Mildenhall, Woodbridge and Upper Heyford.

After a short run-through with a pianist at a prearranged meeting place, you'd set off with the prospect of doing one or two shows like the ones I described we did in Germany. Anyway, the agent in question had heard me on the radio and being somewhat surprised that I was no longer with the act said, 'I was wondering if you'd fancy doing one or two spots on your own?'

My experience of the US floor shows might lead you to think that I'd turn the offer down flat but, as I knew I had to start somewhere and put a stage act together, I said I'd think about it. 'Now listen,' he said, 'I have a show at Bentwaters on Saturday. It's already fully booked but, if you'd like to have a trial run, I'll give you fifteen quid for two spots.' I hung up, and then sat down with a piece of paper, working out a few things I could do – bit of chat here, an Irish song there – until I had about sixteen to twenty minutes ready; enough, I thought, for all emergencies.

He gave me a great welcome on the Saturday and the piano player went through the music which I'd so laboriously written in the meantime. He promised me an extra two quid if I used my own car and took the pianist. 'Okay,' I said and headed for Bentwaters – little did I know what was in store for me.

As I entered the N.C.O. Club, my heart almost stopped – there, hanging on the wall, was a big orange poster: 'To Nite, 9.30 p.m., "The Val Doonican Show" starring Ireland's Top Entertainer Specially Flown Over For The Occasion'.

I turned to the piano player, 'Did you know about this?'

'Yeah, sure,' he replied, 'I honestly thought you were a bit low on music but don't worry, you'll be OK!'

How I got through that show I'll never know. I sang everything – they loved Irish songs, so I did loads of them.

Next morning, the agent rang me. 'I'm told you were fantastic last night, son,' he raved. 'Do you want to do some every weekend? From now on, I'll double the money!' Well, I won't tell you what I called him but I took double the money and within a couple of months my act was really beginning to take shape. I've always believed that if you're going to make mistakes and learn by them, you should try to do it where it won't be noticed too much.

I still never quite knew what was in store for me, so I entered all the clubs with great trepidation. One night I went to a club at Mildenhall where almost all the clientele were black. On that occasion, I found myself billed as 'Ireland's Leading Soul Singer'; you can imagine the thrill 'Scarlet Ribbons' gave them – I was lucky to get out alive.

Fate lent me a hand on another occasion though, at Brize Norton, near Oxford. Heavy snow had fallen all day and I had grave doubts about risking the journey at all. My car was another little Austin A40 and I'd agreed as part of the deal to give someone a lift. When I arrived at rehearsal I was told that the 'someone' I was taking would be a quartet of black singers, called The Manhattan Brothers – two of whom were bigger than my car.

With great misgivings I set off in the driving snow through the West End, on to the A40 road to Oxford – my car bursting at the seams. The Manhattan Brothers were enjoying the snow and tried to reassure me, 'Don't worry, man, it'll be fine.' Well, as it happened, the snow got worse and worse and, pretty soon, there was little if any road to be seen at all. Twice I drove straight on to a roundabout, because I couldn't distinguish it from the snowdrifts, but my good friends just got out, lifted the car, like a dinky toy, back on the road again and off we went.

Thanks to those four guys, we got there, did the show and got home. Next day we discovered that we were the only show that made it that night – to any of the U.S. Bases – and, I'm sure, the only ones who got paid.

I had begun to tackle a few other cabaret jobs by now

and was making my way into the northern circuit of clubs. Manchester had an incredible number who booked live entertainment and, because of the kind of act I did, I tried hard to choose carefully.

I went to a club one night that boasted nonstop entertainment culminating in a star act. The whole evening's entertainment was centred round a wrestling ring and the running order was: wrestling bout – act – wrestling bout – act – tag bout – act and so on for hours. Quite early on I was told to get ready, the wrestling bout ended, the ropes were unclipped, then in I staggered with my amplifier and guitar. The audience, thank God, took me as an opportunity to refill their pint glasses, and I honestly don't think that anybody at all even knew I was there!

By the end of the Anthony Newley tour Lynn and I had, as it were, grown accustomed to each other's faces, so we continued to meet quite regularly when we returned to London. She lived with her mother in a flat at Hendon, and I soon became a constant visitor. Many's the time I would sleep in some makeshift bed huddled up on the kitchen floor – this was about the warmest spot in the apartment which unfortunately had no heating. We'd go for long walks and talk a lot about our respective lives in this strange profession of ours and, even though at that stage we didn't say too much about the future, I think we both had the feeling that something very permanent was on the horizon for us.

It was about that time that the Ramblers were booked for yet another tour to the American bases in Germany. It was only then, really, that I felt the first pangs of love for Lynn – I just didn't want to go. Needless to say I did go and pretty soon was up to my eyes in the old routine – by now, only too familiar to the four of us.

A week or so later found the act both living and working on an Air Force base in a place called Hahn. It was a pretty Godforsaken spot, especially for us civilians, who did not have our activities planned for us day by day. Time crawled by and, hour after hour, I could be found lying on my bed writing endless letters and cards to Lynn.

One chilly afternoon I went for a long walk around the camp area. I simply wanted to kill time taking in a sightseeing tour of the place. Making my way through the rows of prefabricated dwellings, which from the air must have looked like a huge Lego set, my mind was busy with my personal problems.

At a time when wedding bells were ringing in my ears, was I wise to leave the act and try it alone in this precarious profession of mine? Both Lynn and I were 'fatherless', so to speak, which meant that no moral or financial support would be forthcoming in that direction. We were both in our thirties by now, so would I be wiser to find myself something more secure for the future?

I stopped at an intersection to allow a gigantic American car to go by, and there facing me on the corner opposite was a tiny Catholic church. I crossed over. The door was 'on the latch' (as they would say at home in Ireland) so I went in to rest for a bit.

As I whispered my way through a quiet prayer, I could hear the sound of a man's voice gently singing the melody of a popular song of the day. It echoed almost secretly through the tiny building and appeared to be coming from nowhere. Curiosity got the better of me so on tip-toe I made my way up towards the altar rails. I could now tell that the singing was, in fact, coming through the half open door of the little sacristy in the corner. Through the crack in the door I saw, sitting crossed-legged on the floor, a man dressed in fatigue trousers, sweat shirt and gym shoes. He was busily doing some repair work on a piece of fishing tackle, while accompanying himself with his vocal refrain.

He sensed my presence and turned his head, 'Hi there, fella,' he greeted me. 'C'mon in.' So saying, he rose and began to pour some coffee. 'I'm Father Delos, the Catholic chaplain here.' And he handed me the coffee.

I introduced myself, explained what I was doing on the base, and he promised to come along and watch the show one evening.

Within ten minutes or so, we were well into the coffee and he, poor man, was listening to my life-story. Like any good father confessor he summed up my problem:

'If this lady is as lovely as you say and you both want to be together, then you don't want to spend your time thinking about your doubts. Don't wait until you have a million dollars before you make your decision.'

That was all I needed! The rest of the tour just flew by and in no time Lynn and I were making plans. But both of us, strangely enough, had so little time off that we found it extremely difficult to pick a suitable day. We decided on Sunday, 1 April 1962; as I had a radio show on the Monday morning, no honeymoon was possible for the moment – that would have to wait until we could afford it.

Collecting our joint savings together, we put all we had into buying a house. Neither of us felt that it was important to have a posh wedding and we managed without the fancy cars, flowers, cake, and all that. In fact, Lynn and her mother stayed up most of the night making bridge rolls and things, and we invited only our closest friends.

When they had all gone home we settled into our own house and began our life together. The next day I went to the studio to do my radio show, a married man – of less than twenty-four hours. Not very romantic, you might think, but we felt that we had what we wanted: each other and a home that we could afford. Lots of fancy cars and cakes and flowers were to come later.

In July 1963 our first little girl Siobhan had been born. When she was only ten weeks old I was asked to go away to Paris for a month, to entertain the US Forces over there. Lynn and I talked it over and decided that we'd all three go since the weather was so nice. We had a super month, wandering in the parks, round the shops, sitting in

Montmartre watching the artists while we ate huge ice creams. We were proper tourists until night time when, once again, I faced the unpredictable audiences.

In actual fact, the shows were a great success for me and there were no bad ones. To round off my visit, I had a very special show to do.

One of the bases was having a big 'Irish Night' and when the US Army do that, they go to town. They wear green shirts, green hats, they even dye the beer green. There they sit, with huge glasses of what looks like creme de menthe, singing Irish songs. I found it quite remarkable as the Irish themselves never make that kind of fuss and the chances are that there isn't one complete Irishman amongst them.

Seated around a ringside table were six guys, behaving as if they came from Co. Limerick but all looking distinctly Indian (American Indian, that is). They'd had a lot to drink and were very heavy going for the unfortunate comic who preceded me. He was Jewish, very cockney, and his humour escaped them completely. He finally staggered back to the dressing-room, cursing the Irish and the Indians – and wished me all the best.

Things were really noisy so I took the easiest way out and got them singing 'Peg o' my Heart', 'Nelly Kelly', 'When Irish Eyes are Smiling'. Fortunately, my passage was easy and they gave me a thunderous reception – having done most of the work themselves. Still, that's what they wanted and I came off smiling.

My friend the comic, still smarting from his reception when I came into the dressing-room, began to help me with my packing – to speed our departure. Within minutes we were edging our way through the club towards the exit doors.

'Hey! you, Irish!!' We turned to find one of our Indian friends waving us to their table nearby and, try as we might to escape the other way, I knew a visit was inevitable. Briefly, I leaned towards them, 'Thank you, fellas,' I said. 'Have a good party.' Their spokesman stood up, took my arm and offered me a glass of green beer (which was most embarrassing, as I don't even drink the brown stuff), then, putting his other arm round my shoulder and gently shaking me as drunks do, he gazed through his bleary eyes and delivered his tribute, 'You know, Irish, that was the best floor show we've seen here! No!! I really mean it ... you were just wonderful ... and my buddies and I would like you to know, that you're welcome here ... anytime.' At this point, he must have caught my colleague's eye because he suddenly turned his attention to him, 'And you!! my friend ... were just wonderful too ... and we'd like you to come and do a show here ... anytime you want, OK??'

My poor friend couldn't take any more of this insincerity, 'Sure, mate,' he blurted out, 'and anytime you want me here, all you have to do is send up a smoke signal, OK.' With one drunken lurch, the G.I. let go of me and dived at my companion, 'What did you say?' he shouted in a rage, as he stumbled over a table and fell on the floor. My partner disappeared through the exit door at the double while I, trying to be as dignified as possible, walked out. I haven't been back!

Lynn had been on stage since she was twelve years old when she played Cinderella in pantomine – the first engagement of a long and successful career that was to end when she agreed to be my wife. Everybody knows how difficult it is supposed to be to get the theatre out of your blood; so I wondered, from the start, if Lynn could really manage it.

She swears, to this day, that she has not missed it at all, which seems incredible – but, you know, the answer could be this: our work is always a strain and, no matter how long you've been doing it, you worry to some degree about every single show you do. Some people I've met in my career become physically sick before important performances but, in time, learn to accept it as a fact of life.

If, somewhere along the way, they find that they can give it up, the feeling of relief, I'm told, is quite enormous.

Lynn admits now, that she loves the feeling of security which comes from not 'having' to do it any more.

We had been married for about two years when an old agent friend got in touch with her. He was responsible for booking a certain 'room' in the West End where Lynn had worked over the years and was a great favourite. As it happened, he was wondering if, for old time's sake, she might consent to appear there for a month? We talked it over at great length and finally agreed that it might do her good to get back into harness for a few weeks and see how it felt.

At the time, we were living in a very nice semi-detached house in south-east London with our seven-month-old daughter, Siobhan. Together we worked on her act and I was able to help by writing any new music that was required.

When rehearsal day came around I took her to the club and it was wonderful to see her get a warm welcome back from everybody there. I was so glad that she'd decided to do it. Our plan was, as I was only working on the occasional evening, that I would take her to work each night, wait outside in the car while she did her stuff and then take her back home again. Her mother was to look after Siobhan. I had lots of music to write for my radio shows, so I made myself a little portable table that clipped on to my steering whell and, while Lynn was in the club working, I was out in the car doing likewise.

I had a floorshow to do at an American base on the Friday of the first week of Lynn's season, so we arranged a cab for that particular night.

However, it wasn't to be – when Friday came round, I had the most dreadful sore throat. I rang the agent to tell him I couldn't work and, even though he was distressed by my cancelling so late, he could not deny my sincerity when he heard my croaky voice on the phone.

I told Lynn that I could take her to work after all. We sat down and had dinner about 7.30 pm, then we put little Siobhan down for the night and Lynn started to get ready.

Later I sat in my mobile music room outside the restaurant, while Lynn worked as usual. Suddenly, there was a tapping on the car window and I looked up to see the Maitre d'Hotel beckoning me to open my window.

'Sorry to bother you, Val,' he said apologetically, 'but there's a phone call for you at our reception desk.'

'Phone call for me?' I said, surprised. 'Who is it?'

He hesitated for a second or two, 'Ah! it's your doctor, I think,' he replied, shrugging his shoulders.

Puzzled, I removed my music desk and climbed out of the car.

It was, indeed, our family doctor, 'Hello, Val,' he said, rather quietly, 'this is Aubrey. Ah! I just wanted to ask you to come straight home, when Lynn finishes tonight.'

'Is there something wrong?' I asked.

'Well, little Siobhan's not too good ... I'll tell you all about it when you get here,' he replied and hung up.

After the show, Lynn had met some friends inside and wanted me to join them for a drink. I used my sore throat as an excuse for wanting to go straight home but Lynn didn't seem to happy about that, so I had to tell her what Aubrey said. We were very worried.

We drove down the Old Kent Road towards our home without saying very much and, when we eventually turned into the road where we lived, our hearts missed a beat. There, parked outside our house, we saw a police motorcycle.

As we rushed into the house we were greeted by our dear friend, Aubrey, who stood there with tears in his eyes – we both knew, at that moment, that our little girl was dead.

It was what is commonly known nowadays as a 'cot death' and, as Aubrey told us, there was nothing anybody could do about it; she was dead when Lynn's mother went up to make an hourly check on her.

That was the most shattering moment of both our lives and, at the time, it seemed we would never get over it. But, in many ways, I think we learned something very important and it brought us even closer together.

It happened at a time when things were going exceptionally well for me and we could easily have taken all our good fortune for granted. It was almost as if God had reminded us that we should enjoy the good things of life but – never forget that we only have them on loan! He's been extremely generous with His loans ever since.

A striking indication of how things were beginning to change was brought home to me one night in 1964 when I appeared as a star guest at a dance hall in London. I had worked there as one of the boys in the band a few years before since the bandleader was a friend of mine. He had got in touch with me to ask if I was interested in doing a few gigs with his outfit. I was just making my transition from group member to soloist and had no regular income to speak of so , in spite of the fee of only five pounds a night, I said, 'Yes,' feeling that the experience wouldn't do me any harm.

It had been years since I had sat and read bandparts, or sung solo, but I did it for some weeks and enjoyed it although, I must say, the long four-hour sessions were boring now I'd got used to stage performances.

Of course I was an unknown face to the patrons of the dance hall, who didn't take a blind bit of notice of me. They were more interested in dancing and chatting-up their partners. When our interval came round, I'd slip into the back room with the lads, where the owner of the place laid on a few refreshments.

With this in mind, I'll bring you back to 1964 to my guest spot at the same dance hall and continue as a much better known Val Doonican, because of the success of my radio programmes. I was contacted by the owner of that same dance hall, through a mutual friend, who asked me to make a special appearance at his Bank Holiday Dance, for which he'd pay me two hundred pounds. I gladly accepted and went along on the night to find the place packed with customers, eagerly awaiting my arrival.

I was a great success and, on this occasion, had to fight

my way to the little back room afterwards where the doors were locked behind me and the bottles opened. With enthusiasm and gratitude, the owner complimented me on my performance and the resulting audience reaction.

'When can you come back again?' he asked. 'Any Saturday night you're free would suit me.'

I hesitated and said that I'd look at my diary and let him know within a week or so how I was fixed.

'That'll be grand,' he agreed and then, scratching his head and looking puzzled he said, 'You know, I was just saying to one of the lads here, I'm sure I've seen you somewhere before – but I'm damned if I know where!'

I smiled and slowly finished my drink, 'Surely you remember me playing in the band here a couple of years ago.'

He stood there and stared, the palm of his open hand across his forehead, 'Of course,' he hissed through his teeth, 'now I've got you. Well, I'll be damned, what a fiddle!'

I looked in amazement, 'Where's the fiddle?' I stammered. 'A couple of minutes ago you were delighted with everything now, suddenly, it's a fiddle.' I was laughing as I spoke and eventually he, too, saw the funny side of it.

'But how the hell can you be suddenly worth two hundred pounds, when a while ago I got the same thing for a few quid?'

We both smiled wryly as we shook hands. 'Thank you anyway,' I said. 'I don't suppose you'll be wanting me to phone you about the return date!'

'I won't commit myself for the moment,' he grinned, as he stood there, glass in hand, looking like a man who had just won a raffle but couldn't find his ticket.

By 1963 I was enjoying what I considered to be great success working the clubs up north although, in most cases, it involved 'doubling'. This means that you were booked to work two different clubs for the same week. You might be appearing at a club in one part of Manchester,

Leeds or Newcastle, at nine-thirty then, packing your gear into your car, you'd drive to another part of the city, where you would fulfil the other half of your night's work. This was hard graft but, by my standards, the money was very good.

Now one thing I had dearly wanted to do, since about 1960, was to make records. So, armed with some tapes of my radio shows as a kind of audition, I'd attend interviews with several of the bosses of the various companies – all of them listened patiently to me and to my tapes but, the answer was always the same, 'We don't think there would be a demand for your style of singing in the present-day market.'

I must say I quite understood how they felt about it and I'm sure, had I been in their position, viewing the material in the charts, I wouldn't have taken the gamble either! I shelved my tapes for the moment and just got on with my radio and cabaret work having no idea that, in the very near future, my life would be dramatically changed by a sequence of events which, I think you'll agree, sound like a fairy tale.

My work was now being handled by one of the country's leading agents and managers, Evelyn Taylor, a lady who made international stars out of Adam Faith and Sandie Shaw, as well as many others and who was to guide my career brilliantly for the next twenty years. Knowing that I had this aspect of my career under control helped me to concentrate more than ever on the artistic side. Eve rang me one day to say she'd had a call from David Jacobs who, aside from his TV and radio work, spent much of his time as a leading light in the running of the charitable group Stars Organisation for Spastics or 'S.O.S.'

David was organising a big Charity Concert at the De La Ware Pavilion, Bexhill-on-Sea and, to my great pleasure, wanted me to appear on the same bill as people like Vera Lynn, Dickie Henderson, Frankie Vaughan and a host of others. The reason for Davis's interest was that he had become aware of the popularity of my radio show even though, he admitted, he had no idea what I looked like or what my performance would be like.

I agreed to do the show and travelled down to Bexhill on the Sunday afternoon to rehearse in preparation for the big evening. My spot in the show came immediately after the opening music and my allocated time was ten minutes. The audience was lovely and my part of the show went fine. I returned to my dressing-room where I had a meal provided by the organisers before journeying home. I couldn't stay for the festivities planned for the late evening, because I had an early radio show the next morning.

I was interrupted by a tapping on my door and before I could speak with my mouth full, the unexpected visitor popped his head into the room – it was Dickie Henderson.

'Hi there,' he said.

I stood up and shook hands with him.

'You know,' he went on, 'I've just been standing at the back of the theatre watching you, you were great!'

'Thank you very much,' I replied, delighted with myself but not quite sure of what to say – I'd never had a compliment from a star before.

Dickie was in a hurry so, as he left the room he said, 'Quite honestly, I'd never heard of you before but, you've got it – and I'll say this – if you're not a star this time next year, there's no justice in show business.'

Well, what can you say to that? I couldn't make up my mind whether it was a lot of old flannel, or not, while at the same time I told myself that he didn't need to come around to my room if he didn't mean it.

Soon, I was on my way home feeling very satisfied with my night's work. Lynn woke up when I came in and I told her she'd better be prepared for the fact that, very soon, she would be sleeping with a star! We've laughed about that, many times.

The following week I was booked to do a week's cabaret at the Piccadilly Club in Manchester City Centre and one of the things I had to do, before making the trip, was to have my hair cut. It was my usual practice to have it done at the Barber's Shop in the Piccadilly Hotel in London, whenever I was in town and I rang the barber, Jack Lee, and went in on the Wednesday.

While Jack was cutting my hair and we were indulging in the usual hairdresser-customer chit chat, he suddenly changed the subject, 'Oh! by the way,' he said, looking at me in the mirror, 'I had a fan of yours in here yesterday.'

'Really,' I replied. 'Who was it, Marilyn Monroe?'

'No, seriously,' said Jack waving his comb about, 'it was Dickie Henderson – said he was going to tell Val Parnell about you – loved your act on Sunday night.' So, it wasn't the old flannel, he did mean it!

It was at this stage that things began to fall into place. The very next day the man sitting in that barber's chair was, in fact, Val Parnell – probably the greatest impresario this country had and the man responsible for, among other things, the TV show 'Sunday Night At The London Palladium'. As Jack was cutting his hair, he related the story about Dickie and myself. Mr Parnell said he hadn't heard of me but showed interest.

As for me, I went off to Manchester at the weekend and booked into my digs for the week. The manager of the club, Jerry Harris, quite staggered me, midweek, by telling me that a gentleman named Alec Fyne was in town and would be popping in for a few minutes. Now this particular gentleman, belive it or not, happened to be Val Parnell's talent scout and booking manager and, at that time, knew absolutely nothing about the 'barber's shop quartet'. He sat and watched me, while he ate and had a drink and, afterwards, sent me his compliments.

Next day on his return to London, he mentioned me to Val Parnell who, by now, was becoming sufficiently interested to ask where I was working next, in case he decided to come and have a look for himself.

The following week was perfect: I was at 'The Jack of Clubs', a restaurant owned by a family called Isow, which was situated right in the heart of Soho. I was appearing there, once nightly, at about eleven-fifteen. Somebody up there loved me again that week, for on Monday, Tuesday and Wednesday, the audience were not very interested but – on Thursday, they were wonderful. Mr Parnell chose to have a look at me on the Thursday.

My performance was as good as I could make it and I had nothing whatever to complain about. After I'd finished, I had a message that the great man wanted to speak to me. He was so charming to me and not at all like the impresarios you see in the movies – none of the 'I'm gonna make you a star' bit or anything like that, just a straightforward compliment. 'You were great tonight,' he said smiling, 'very refreshing stuff. I think you'd do well on "Sunday Night at the Palladium".'

'What!' I said, sitting bolt upright. 'Are you serious?'

He turned to Alec Fyne who was with him at the table, 'What vacant dates have we got, Alec?' he asked.

After a quick flick through his diary, Alec Fyne suggested the last Sunday in May or the first Sunday in June.

Mr Parnell looked at me, 'What do you say then?'

'Oh!' I said, 'yes, I can do both those Sundays.' It was meant to be a silly joke, from an embarrassed but very excited man. As it turned out – I did both those Sundays.

Arriving at the Palladium on that momentous day, my music under my arm (which I'd done myself and had vetted by Ken Thorne), I wondered who to approach in the hubbub of such an important occasion.

I needn't have worried, however, as everybody on the staff, from George Cooper the doorman through to the stage manager, looked straight past me, threw their arms up in welcome and shouted, 'Lynn! How lovely to see you. What are you doing here?'

Lynn, who had done a long season there a few years earlier, introduced her husband to all her friends backstage and, before I knew it, I was one of the family. I did my rehearsal – still getting lots of encouragement from my new-found guardian angel, Mr Parnell.

Afterwards, as I sat in my room on the threshold of all sorts of incredible things, my door opened and he came in but didn't sit down. 'Well, I must be off now, Val,' he said. 'I always like to watch the show at home.'

I thanked him for everything he had done and hoped it would come over OK. He offered his hand to me, 'Just be yourself,' he told me, 'and tomorrow, I think you'll be a star.'

That may sound very 'Hollywood' on paper but it didn't sound that way to me and, the nice thing was, that there was so much truth in his prediction. Within a week, I had been invited back to the Palladium, been offered a choice of recording contracts and lots of television work.

'What do you think I should do?' I asked Eve, my manager.

'Nothing,' she said. 'You and Lynn have a holiday – and think hard what you'd like to do yourself. It will all still be there, when you get back.' She was right ... it was!

MARY

by Patricia Collins

A CHILD YOU'LL WANT
TO REMEMBER.

Mary Collins was a really beautiful baby. Born
prematurely, she had a tiny oval face, a rosebud mouth
and an enchanting smile. The third child of parents who
came from the bustle of New York to make a home in
Ireland, Mary found a warm and secure place in the heart
of the family.

**Then, eight months later, Patricia Collins learned
that Mary was brain damaged. Doctors diagnosed
cerebral palsy; she would probably never walk
and she would almost certainly be retarded.**

The shock of this discovery plunged Patricia into despair.
Mary needed extensive therapy and the burden of caring
for her increased Patricia's growing resentment and guilt
– she began to drink heavily, blaming herself for what
had happened. When circumstances forced the Collins
family to return to America, Patricia made a wrenching
decision to leave Mary behind in Ireland in a residential
home for two years. The years in Ireland did nothing to
lessen the severity of Mary's disabilities, but another kind
of change did occur. Mary was becoming a determined,
courageous child with a winning personality and she
gave a very special purpose and meaning to life.

This is an intimate, inspiring and deeply moving account
of a mother's journey from despair to joy and of the
power of the human spirit to overcome adversity through
love and understanding.

A STORY YOU WON'T FORGET.

BIOGRAPHY   0 7221 2482 1   £1.50

WILL

The remarkable autobiography of

G. GORDON LIDDY

WHAT MADE LIDDY KEEP SILENCE WHEN HIS
FELLOW WATERGATE CONSPIRATORS WERE
PREPARED TO TALK? WHAT MADE LIDDY
PREPARED TO KILL E. HOWARD HUNT AND
NEWSPAPER COLUMNIST JACK ANDERSON?
WHAT MADE LIDDY OFFER TO BE
ASSASSINATED? WHAT MAKES HIM SUCH AN
EXTRAORDINARY MAN?
READ *WILL* AND YOU'LL FIND OUT . . .

G. Gordon Liddy's refusal to talk about his role
in Watergate resulted in a prison sentence of
twenty years. After serving nearly five years,
President Carter reduced Liddy's sentence. Now
Liddy is a free man. And now he is prepared to
reveal the truth.

'What is most striking about WILL is what it
reveals about the kind of man who will do
anything to stop those he sees as his country's
enemies' *Time*

AUTOBIOGRAPHY   0 7221 5550 6   £1.75

A SELECTION OF BESTSELLERS FROM **SPHERE**

FICTION

I, SAID THE SPY	Derek Lambert	£1.75	☐
HEART OF WAR	John Masters	£1.95	☐
REVELATIONS	Phyllis Naylor	£1.50	☐
LOVING	Danielle Steel	£1.50	☐

FILM & TV TIE-INS

MUPPET MANNERS	Pat Relf	95p	☐
FOZZIE'S BIG BOOK OF SIDE-SPLITTING JOKES	Pat Relf	95p	☐
THE PROFESSIONALS	Ken Blake	£1.00	
SERIES		each	☐

NON-FICTION

A WAY TO DIE	Rosemary & Victor Zorza	£1.50	☐
MARY	Patricia Collins	£1.50	☐
THE CLASSIFIED MAN	Susanna M. Hoffman	£1.50	☐
WILL	G. Gordon Liddy	£1.75	☐
ROGET'S THESAURUS		£2.10	☐

All Sphere Books are available at your local bookshop or newsagent, or can be ordered direct from the publisher. Just tick the titles you want and fill in the form below.

Name ⎯⎯⎯⎯⎯⎯⎯⎯⎯⎯⎯⎯⎯⎯⎯⎯⎯⎯⎯

Address ⎯⎯⎯⎯⎯⎯⎯⎯⎯⎯⎯⎯⎯⎯⎯⎯

⎯⎯⎯⎯⎯⎯⎯⎯⎯⎯⎯⎯⎯⎯⎯⎯⎯⎯⎯⎯

Write to Sphere Books, Cash Sales Department, P.O. Box 11, Falmouth, Cornwall TR10 9EN.

Please enclose a cheque or postal order to the value of the cover price:

UK: 40p for the first book, 18p for the second book and 13p for each additional book ordered to a maximum charge of £1.49.

OVERSEAS: 60p for the first book plus 18p per copy for each additional book.

BFPO & EIRE: 40p for the first book, 18p for the second book plus 13p per copy for the next 7 books, thereafter 7p per book.

Sphere Books reserve the right to show new retail prices on covers which may differ from those previously advertised in the text or elsewhere, and to increase postal rates in accordance with the PO.